# Evolving Learner

**Lainie**

*For my amazing husband, Lawrence, and his unwavering faith in me.*
*For Kendall and Blake, my blessings.*

*For my parents, who lovingly taught me the importance of hard work and perseverance.*

**Kristy**

*For my hubby, Matt, thank you for the time and space you give me*
*and allowing me to pursue my passions.*

*For Micah, you are my world, kid.*

*For my fur babies, thank you for always being next to me when I write.*
*Your comfort helped me to push through.*

**Lauren**

*For my husband and best friend, James, your unending support, wit,*
*and humor carry me through everything, every day!*

*For Jack and Henry—You Are My Sunshine—love you more!*

*For my parents, you always taught me to pursue a goal and*
*never stop learning. You would have loved this, Mom!*

# Evolving Learner

## Shifting From Professional Development to Professional Learning From Kids, Peers, and the World

**Lainie Rowell**
**Kristy Andre**
**Lauren Steinmann**

*Foreword by Thomas C. Murray*

A Joint Publication

CORWIN *learningforward*

A SAGE Publishing Company

FOR INFORMATION:

Corwin

A SAGE Company

2455 Teller Road

Thousand Oaks, California 91320

(800) 233-9936

www.corwin.com

SAGE Publications Ltd.

1 Oliver's Yard

55 City Road

London EC1Y 1SP

United Kingdom

SAGE Publications India Pvt. Ltd.

B 1/I 1 Mohan Cooperative Industrial Area

Mathura Road, New Delhi 110 044

India

SAGE Publications Asia-Pacific Pte. Ltd.

18 Cross Street #10-10/11/12

China Square Central

Singapore 048423

Program Director and Publisher:   Dan Alpert

Senior Content Development
   Editor:   Lucas Schleicher

Associate Content Development
   Editor:   Mia Rodriguez

Production Editor:   Amy Schroller

Copy Editor:   Teresa Herlinger

Typesetter:   C&M Digitals (P) Ltd.

Proofreader:   Susan Schon

Indexer:   Sheila Hill

Cover and Graphic Designer:   Scott Van Atta

Marketing Manager:   Sharon Pendergast

Printed in the United States of America

ISBN 978-1-5443-3832-3

SUSTAINABLE FORESTRY INITIATIVE   Certified Sourcing
www.sfiprogram.org
SFI-00756

This book is printed on acid-free paper.

20 21 22 23 24 10 9 8 7 6 5 4 3 2 1

# CONTENTS

**CHAPTER THREE**

# LEARNING FROM THE WORLD    124

# FOREWORD

## THOMAS C. MURRAY

It was February of my second year as an elementary principal when it started to become clear to me. That morning, Suzie, one of the greatest teachers that I've ever worked with, came running into my office. She was smiling from ear to ear as she handed me her professional development checklist of hours required by her teacher contract. *"I finished yesterday, Tom! I went to my last workshop and I finished my 18 hours for the year. Woohoo! I'm finished with my professional development for the year!"* Wanting to show my support for one of my amazing teachers, I gave her a high five and told her how proud of her I was. I told her how I appreciated the way she was always on the ball and ahead of the game. It was part of who she was.

When I say that she was an amazing teacher, I don't say that lightly. When in her classroom, I'd watch in amazement. She had such a way about her. Her kids loved her and excelled year after year. Each summer, dozens of parent requests would come through for her, and I knew exactly why. She was a far better teacher than I ever was. Her positive attitude and can-do mindset radiated, and she found a way to do it all. She was the exact kind of teacher I wanted for my own children.

Driving home that afternoon, I began to reflect on our brief conversation. As you might anticipate, Suzie was the kind of teacher who, if something was required to be completed by June, would have it finished in February. Being a master of her craft, she was always leading the way. As I drove, I kept hearing her words, *"Woohoo! I finished my professional development for the year!"* repeat over and over in my mind. I reflected upon my leadership in reinforcing that mindset and how the typical end-of-the-year evaluation conversations I'd have with my team did as well. Having a teacher contract that required 18 hours per year of professional development outside of the school day, the conversations often sounded like this:

*"Here are the workshops that I went to this year . . ."*

*"Here are the hours that I earned . . ."*

*"My 18 hours were completed by . . ."*

My heart began to sink. As the principal, I was reinforcing an ineffective system—a system that cared more about seat time than it did about actual growth. It's the exact reason why I shared in my first book that, *"When we measure seat time, we measure the wrong end of the learner."* What does seat time tell us about growth or effectiveness? Nothing. It tells us where a person was on Earth at a given time. Like so many others, we had created a system where even our very best people were more concerned about checking off the required hours than they were about growing from the experiences, and our supervision procedures created and reinforced that mindset.

Consider the following scenarios:

**Scenario 1:** *Paisley, a fourth-grade teacher, shows up early for the September inservice day. Upon walking through the school doors, she's greeted with the teacher sign-in sheets to verify her attendance. She picks up her schedule for the day and goes to the required four sessions planned for her. At the end of the last session, she says goodbye to a few colleagues and leaves for the day. A few days later, she's emailed her certificate of attendance, verifying her hours earned.*

**Scenario 2:** *Caden, a high school teacher, is excited for the first EdCamp that's occurring in his area on Saturday. After meeting a few of his colleagues for coffee, they travel over to a neighboring high school together. Caden and his teammates spend the first hour of the day networking and connecting with other educators from the surrounding area. Throughout the day, Caden helps to facilitate a session on social-emotional learning; participates in another session on designing learner-centered spaces; and joins two others on the effective use of technology, an area that he's looking to grow professionally. The following Monday, Caden shares the experience* *with his principal and receives a response of, "That's wonderful! I'm glad you enjoyed it. But, unfortunately, that won't count for your professional development hours this year. You know that, right?"*

Do these fictional scenarios sound familiar?

Having the privilege of leading professional learning for thousands of educators each year, from superintendents and principals to teachers and support staff, I've asked well over 10,000 educators to reflect on their experience around the following two questions:

*What is the best professional learning you've ever experienced? What characteristics made it the best?*

*What is the worst professional learning you've ever experienced? What characteristics made it the worst?*

What's fascinating to me is that no matter the audience, and no matter the title on one's business cards, the responses are almost always identical. After sharing their experiences in small groups, I'll survey the audience to define the characteristics. They always sound something like this:

**Best Experiences:** *Relevant, engaging, interactive, collaborative, fun, practical, challenging, ongoing, dynamic presenter, had voice and choice, included follow-up*

**Worst Experiences:** *Irrelevant for my position, sit and get, death by PowerPoint, boring presenter, no engagement, no choice, minimal follow-up*

Do these characteristics sound familiar when compared with your best and worst experiences? I'm guessing so.

Here's the secret around effective professional learning: It's not a secret at all. So much evidence points to the fact that high-quality professional learning parallels high-quality teaching and learning, and today, I'm filled with hope. Many school and district leaders have been shifting the paradigm from top-down, one-size-fits-all, sit-and-get, hours-based accountability to a model that actually works—a model where professional learning isn't done to educators, but one in which they are a vital part; a model of ownership and growth, not simply a checklist of required hours; a model such as the one outlined in the following pages.

There's a video that I often use with educators entitled *Stuck on an Escalator*. I encourage you to check it out on YouTube. In the video, two strangers step on an escalator and about halfway up, the escalator comes to an unexpected stop. Being the only two on the escalator in what appears to be an empty building, the two strangers begin to ponder what to do next, ultimately crying out for anyone who may be able to help. Although many analogies can be made regarding owning the solution to a problem, in my opinion, the analogies around professional learning are vast. If we wait for others to do it for us, the impact will be negligible. When we take ownership of our own learning, and our lens shifts to fully see what's possible, the path forward becomes visible.

When we reflect further on the scenario from the video above, it's important to understand how the answer was in front of them the entire time. When we compare professional learning to a student learning paradigm, as the authors do in this book, we are forced to reflect on our own practice. As educators, how long have we been talking about differentiated learning for students? Twenty years? How long have we talked about students owning their work? How many times did I, as a school or district leader, lead sessions in the exact opposite way from how I was expecting my teachers to lead in the classroom?

I'm sure you get the point. If we lead it, we must model it. If we expect it, we must model it. If we value it, we must find a way to make it happen. When we do, amazing things occur. When we value a traditional process, we'll get traditional results. When we value nontraditional experiences, such as those you'll read about in this text, we'll get nontraditional outcomes—outcomes that will benefit both students and those who lead them.

I'm really excited about the incredible book that you are about to read. In fact, it's the exact type of book I wish I had had access to early in my educational career, as it would have guided my mindset and allowed me to be more effective in leading the work. Whether you're a classroom teacher, instructional coach, building principal, or a district-level leader, authors Rowell, Andre, and Steinmann will take you on a journey and offer various supports along the way, to shift from traditional professional development to evidence-based professional learning that works! They'll help you learn, unlearn, and relearn while offering a new lens as an evolving learner to *focus, learn, refine, and reflect.* The authors will help open doors that you may have feared in the past while sharing practical tips to implement and steps to take during the change process.

The work is hard, but our kids are worth it.

You are part of the solution! Together, we can do this!

All for the kids we serve,

Thomas C. Murray
@thomascmurray
Director of Innovation, Future Ready Schools®
Washington, D.C.

# ACKNOWLEDGMENTS

**From the Team**

> "I not only use all the brains that I have, but all the brains I can borrow."
>
> —Woodrow Wilson

*Evolving Learning* represents a 3-year journey to discover the best in professional learning, but more importantly, it represents the power of professional learning through relationships. Every book, journal, and article we read; every video we watched; every podcast we listened to in researching for this book, all of it was in some way connected to our own learning from kids, peers, and the world, and we would like to thank as many of those key people as possible.

First, we would like to thank the amazing Robert Craven for bringing the three of us together as a writing team. We would also like to thank our publisher for supporting us through this process. Self-publishing was an option, and we were momentarily tempted to go that route, but we are forever grateful that we followed our collective gut and chose Corwin, a respected publisher, to guide us and bring the very best out of us. In particular, Dan Alpert and Lucas Schleicher are the best "critical friends" you could have. Their deep knowledge of education and professional learning as well as their insights and perspectives had a profound impact on this book. We would also like to thank Teresa Herlinger, our exceptional copy editor, who was incredibly quick yet thorough, as well as kind and respectful in providing thoughtful feedback. Another Corwin team member that I, Lainie, want to acknowledge is Ariel Bartlett, who first approached me about writing this book. Ariel's ability to read the education landscape and identify the need to build capacity in professional learning ignited this entire journey. Last but not least on the Corwin team, we have always been passionate about the design of this book and we want to thank the Corwin design team, in particular, Scott Van Atta, for listening to our ideas and then making them even better. We also want to thank Paul Reynolds, who generously shared his time, experience, and wisdom during the production stage.

Thank you to Tom Murray, whose vision for transforming learning as well as his integrity and core values made him the first and only person on our list to write the foreword of this book. Tom is deeply committed to what is best for all learners (kids and adults), and he works tirelessly on their behalf. The way he leads with compassion and humility is unparalleled. We are eternally grateful to him for his contribution to this book.

We would also like to thank all of the learners (kids and adults) who shared their stories throughout this book:

| | |
|---|---|
| Kennedy Dirkes | Adora Svitak |
| Jeremy Hersch | Ronelle Swart |
| Eric Marcos | Megan Waddell Trimnal |
| Melissa Marshall | Tashi Widmer |
| Andrew Stadel | |

Finally, our team would like to acknowledge some of the key thought leaders who helped us form our thinking:

| | |
|---|---|
| Elena Aguilar | Robert J. Marzano |
| Brené Brown | Eric Mazur |
| Linda Darling-Hammond | Sugata Mitra |
| Michael Fullan | Dan Pink |
| John Hattie | Mitchel Resnick |
| Austin Kleon | Sir Ken Robinson |
| Jim Knight | Simon Sinek |

## Lainie

I have had countless teachers and mentors (kids and adults) who have inspired me throughout my career. This is an attempt to highlight at least some of those people.

To begin, thank you to my colleagues at Orange County Department of Education for pushing me to keep my perspective broad while also thinking deeply—in particular, Dr. Christine Olmstead, whose ability to see a challenge from every angle and come up with comprehensive, innovative solutions that best serves both kid learners and adult learners is a constant inspiration to me.

Thank you to my brilliant mentor, Alan November, and all of my Building Learning Communities (BLC) friends who have stretched my thinking over the years, especially Brian Mull, Jennifer Bowden, Dan November, Mike Gorman, Chris Long, Caitlin Krause, Sara Wilkie, Ewan McIntosh, Shannon McClintock Miller, Tracy Sockalosky, Darren Kuropatwa, Joy Kirr, Stacey Roshan, Marcy Reed, Jim Wenzloff, Chris Burnett, Amy Burvall, Tom Daccord, Marco Torres, and the Alas Media crew to name just a few. Thank you also to Kristin Ziemke, who was completely honest with me about how hard it is to write a book and simultaneously encouraged me to do it.

To the CUE community and those who served on the CUE board with me, in particular Robert Craven and Ray Chavez, your leadership helped shape my understanding of community and learning relationships. Thank you to Mike Lawrence who served as CUE's CEO during my time on the board. Mike is a master in connecting people and ideas. He is always looking to lift people up, and he connected me to countless thought leaders. Mike was also the driving force behind Leading Edge Certification and my leadership role in the program, an experience that opened my eyes to a whole world of innovative approaches to learning design for adults.

Thank you to my Apple family, the amazing community of Apple Distinguished Educators who are constantly sharing new ideas as well as the dedicated Apple Professional Learning team that I traveled with, learned with, and laughed with for many years.

Thank you to my fellow Google Certified Innovators and in particular, Dr. Mark Wagner, for challenging my thinking and giving me endless opportunities to grow in my practice.

To my friends at BloomBoard, Allison Powell, Edward Vandenberg, Kelly Montes De Oca, and Jason Lange, you are the epitome of evolving learners, constantly iterating, making it impossible to keep up with you, but I will keep trying.

I spent 15 years in Newport-Mesa USD, and I am so very grateful to Dr. Monique Huibregtse and Steven Glyer for modeling exceptional leadership, having faith in me, and putting me on an education leadership pathway.

Thank you to my dear and creative friend, Allyson Smith Liu, for helping me as I was initially trying to articulate the concept of this book. She suggested the phrase, "Evolving Learner" and designed the Evolving Learner graphic in the Introduction. I would also like to thank another dear and creative friend, Jennifer Hoover, for inspiring me to visually tell stories in simple and beautiful ways.

Thank you to Colleen Gurney, an exceptional educator and lifelong friend as well as the most amazing teaching partner anyone could ever ask for. Sharing a classroom with Colleen and watching her teach was a true gift. I learned so much, and it helped me understand the power of seeing peers in practice.

To Kristy and Lauren, my coauthors and friends, this has been the best professional learning experience of my life. Thank you for putting up with me!

Last, but not least, to the precious little ones who I have been blessed to learn with throughout my career, your families entrust me, as your teacher, to help you learn, but it has always been reciprocal, and I'm forever grateful for everything you teach me.

### Kristy

School has always been a safe place for me. Thank you to all my teachers who created that safe space. Thank you to Mr. Robert Clements for modeling the type of teacher that I always wanted to be.

Thank you to all the incredible leaders I have had the opportunity to work with: Dr. Gregory Franklin, Kathie Nielson, Dr. Maggie Villegas, Chris Matos, Dr. Grant Litfin, Robert Craven, Dr. Crystal Turner, Mindy Smith, Deanna Parks, Katy Sheyka, Mic Shakelford, Dr. Dustin O'Malley, Garrett Kerr, and Sisanda Siboto. Thank you to all my colleagues who have allowed me to evolve and have inspired me to be more.

Thank you to all the amazing leaders I have been able to learn from, including my USC dissertation chairs, Dr. Pedro Garcia and Dr. Rudy Castruita.

To Lainie and Lauren, what a journey it has been. Thank you for your passion and drive and your willingness to evolve together.

To my students, those that I have taught online, in class, or in South Africa, thank you for allowing me to learn from all of you. You have shaped me into the person I am now. I am forever grateful to each of you, and I am so glad we were able to cross paths in our learning journeys.

**Lauren**

I had the immense privilege of not only attending amazing schools growing up, but working in amazing schools during my career.

Thank you to my amazing teachers and professors. From kindergarten to college to graduate school, I have been blessed, and I am so grateful.

Even when I have been the teacher or principal, I am still always a student. Thank you to all of my students, each and every one of you. I have learned so much and continue to grow from you each and every day!

Thank you to the amazing district that hired me right out of my credential program and has continued to help me grow, learn, evolve, and thrive in ways I could never have imagined. So many opportunities lie in saying "yes" to the unknown. The colleagues I work with have taught me so much and bring so much friendship and joy into my life. Thank you to Dr. Greg Franklin, Maggie Villegas, Kathie Nielsen, Dr. Grant Litfin, Dr. Crystal Turner, Garrett Kerr, Gerry Aust, Janet Bittick, Chris Gregg, Robert Craven, and so many more. These leaders took chances on me, push me to be the best version of myself, and make me dig deeper to help others.

To Lainie and Kristy, what an amazing journey! Our crazy adventure continues to bring fun opportunities, but the friendship is the icing on the cake.

Finally, a note about my amazing mom, Carolyn McInerney. She was an advocate for kids and worked in so many capacities to bring about change in schools and bring a better quality of life to everyone. I learned from her each and every day and strive to honor her work—and memory—every day.

# PUBLISHER'S ACKNOWLEDGMENTS

Corwin gratefully acknowledges the contributions of the following reviewers:

Dr. Sammie Cervantez
Principal
Shell Beach Elementary School
Pismo Beach, CA

Claudia Danna
Adjunct Professor, Educational
    Consultant, Teacher Coach
Sacred Heart University/Griswold
    Public Schools
Griswold, CT

Linda Diaz
Secondary Transition Specialist and
    Parent Liaison
Monroe County School District
Sugarloaf Key, FL

Robert Evans, EdD
Director of Teaching & Learning
American International School of
    Johannesburg
Johannesburg, South Africa

Katina Keener
Principal
Achilles Elementary
Hayes, VA

Patti J. Larche
Director of Curriculum and
    Instruction
Phelps-Clifton Springs School
    District
Clifton Springs, NY

Beth Madison
Principal
Robert Gray Middle School
Portland, OR

Jacie Maslyk
Assistant Superintendent
Hopewell Area School District
Aliquippa, PA

Melissa Miller
Sixth-Grade Science Teacher
Farmington Middle School
Farmington, AR

Cheryl Steel Oakes
Resource Room Teacher
Wells Ogunquit Community School
    District
Wells, ME

Debra Paradowski
Administrator
Arrowhead Union High School
Hartland, WI

Renee Peoples
Instructional Coach
Swain County Schools
Bryson City, NC

Kelly VanLaeken
Director of Curriculum, Instruction,
  and Assessment
Gananda Central School District
Walworth, NY

Ron Whalen
Director of Digital Teaching and
  Learning
Durham Public Schools
Durham, NC

# ABOUT THE AUTHORS

**Lainie Rowell** is an educator and international speaker. Her areas of expertise include professional learning, community building, and designing innovative learning experiences. During her 22 years in education, Lainie has taught elementary, secondary, and higher education. She also served in a district-level leadership position supporting 22,000 students and 1,200 teachers at 33 schools. As a consultant, Lainie's client list ranges from Fortune 100 companies like Apple and Google to school districts and independent schools. Lainie is a TEDx speaker with more than 15 years of experience presenting at local, regional, and international conferences including Building Learning Communities (BLC) and the Leadership 3.0 Symposium. Since 2014, Lainie has been a consultant for Orange County Department of Education's Institute for Leadership Development facilitating professional learning for administrators. Learn more about Lainie at lainierowell.com.

**Kristy Andre, EdD** is an educator who is always thinking of ways to evolve and grow and hopes to always provide a space for everyone to feel loved, cared for, and safe. She has a master's in education from Concordia University, Irvine, and a doctorate in educational leadership from the University of Southern California. Kristy has served as an elementary teacher, middle school teacher, and instructional coach. She has taught in a traditional classroom setting, a nontraditional classroom setting, and in South Africa for 2 years. Kristy also serves as an adjunct professor where she teaches in the Master's in Educational Technology program. Learn more about Dr. Kristy Andre at kristyandre.com.

**Lauren Steinmann, EdD** is an educator, administrator, and lifelong learner who is passionate about helping students and teachers thrive in their school communities and in the world. She has taught multiple elementary grades and served as a Digital Learning Coach and Teacher on Special Assignment in STEM and currently works as an elementary principal in Southern California. Lauren holds a master's in educational administration from Concordia

University and a doctorate in educational leadership from the University of Southern California. Lauren loves meeting and connecting with educators from around the world and sharing her love of learning as a presenter and speaker at conferences including CA STEAM Symposium, LEAD3, EdTalk, NGSS Rollout, Cotsen STEAM Ahead, and CUE Conferences. Find Dr. Lauren Steinmann on Twitter: @LaurenMStein.

# INTRODUCTION

"There are only two ways to influence human behavior: You can manipulate or you can inspire it."

—Simon Sinek

The three of us have spent a combined 48 years as educators. We have participated in and provided "professional development" countless times. We have seen the best and worst of teacher learning. We set out to write together not because we had all the answers, but rather, because we wanted answers. We wanted to curate the most innovative, effective, and sustainable approaches to improving our practice and the practice of all educators.

As we share what we have learned, we carefully choose when we use two terms, *professional development* and *professional learning*. When we use the term *professional development*, or *PD*, we are talking about "sit and get" workshop design, which is traditionally externally driven and one-size-fits-all. When we use the term *professional learning*, or *PL*, we are talking about personalized experiences that focus on goals and outcomes, not seat time. In other words, we want to be continuously improving, and we want learner agency for adults, just as we want learner agency for kids.

At the time of this writing, there are states, counties, districts, and schools using the term professional development, or PD, even though they have evolved to innovative professional learning practices. While we (and many others) are intentional in using the words "professional learning," simply using the phrase "professional development" does not necessarily reflect the mindset and practices of those educators. The reality is that it goes much deeper than semantics. It is about a paradigm shift where educators take ownership of their own learning, becoming adaptive experts to keep up with a fast-changing world. It is about personalized adult learning experiences, and this requires careful planning that is focused on the goal of positive growth in learner outcomes while respecting the adult learner every step of the way.

# PD vs. PL

| | |
|---|---|
| TRADITIONAL | INNOVATIVE |
| EXTERNALLY DRIVEN | LEARNER DRIVEN |
| ONE-SIZE-FITS-ALL | PERSONALIZED |
| SEAT TIME | DELIVERABLES |

In short, we are advocates for respecting *all* learners, and we believe that respecting the adult learner and personalizing professional learning for all is a disruptor that will lead to the same shift in classrooms.

Another phrase we chose carefully is "evolving learner." We believe that as educators it is our responsibility to be lifelong learners, and we also need to continue to learn *how* to learn. The ways in which we can learn are evolving at an unprecedented rate, which is why it is imperative that we continue to learn how to learn. For example, Twitter has only been around since 2006, yet today, many couldn't imagine professional learning without this tool. While the tools will come and go, the purpose of the tool will most likely endure. Years ago, there was a very popular social network that all the "kids" were using called MySpace. (One of us may have even met her husband there.) Eventually, it was replaced in popularity by Facebook and a host of other social networking services, but the purpose of connecting people endures. In other words, it isn't about the tools; it is about the relationships the tools enable.

## IT ISN'T ABOUT THE TOOLS; IT IS ABOUT THE RELATIONSHIPS THE TOOLS ENABLE.

In addition to the seemingly endless options for sharing and learning through networks, we are also evolving into a more on-demand culture. Pacing the masses—forcing everyone to go at the exact same pace—is simply becoming less and less acceptable. Who could forget the first time their favorite show was released on Netflix all at once—an entire season available to watch when and where you want! In the classroom, we have seen more learner choice in pacing thanks to blended and online learning and other innovative practices, but we rarely see choice in pacing given to educators.

Learning Forward has developed Standards for Professional Learning that outline the critical elements in today's professional learning that lead to "effective teaching practices, supportive leadership, and improved student results" (learningforward.org). These standards clearly define what professional learning should look like, and this book is a practitioner's guide to mastering those standards by leveraging learning relationships in a cycle of inquiry. It is time for professional development to evolve to professional learning!

# UNLEARN, THEN RELEARN

Futurist Alvin Toffler wrote in his 1970 book *Future Shock,* "The illiterate of the 21st century will not be those who cannot read and write, but those who cannot learn, unlearn and relearn." This book advocates for us, as educators, to evolve by continuing to learn how to learn, and it is important to note that unlearning is also critical. Without question, unlearning is hard, especially in a system as resilient as education. After all, most of us spent our formative years with a teacher at the front of the room while we remained seated in carefully lined-up rows, waiting to receive and absorb information. Is it any wonder that our traditional system has resisted all sorts of attempts to reform it, when the system is largely run by those who are successful products of it?

Not only is unlearning hard, but it can be even harder than learning. Chris Dede, professor at the Harvard Graduate School of Education, says, "Intellectually, you get it and you want to do it, because you want to be successful, but emotionally and socially, it's very, very difficult for you to change because you're making a fundamental change to your identity (Will, 2019, n.p.).

As we will explore throughout this book, learning from kids, peers, and the world gives us the social and emotional support to be strong enough to be vulnerable. A *cycle of inquiry* provides a structure to challenge our beliefs through action research. The two combined give us the capacity to learn, unlearn, and relearn as needed. We will almost certainly fail along the way, but that is a natural part of this messy, nonlinear, and sometimes scary process.

To be clear, we know this is a definite shift from traditional education. We are advocating for changing structures, and we are advocating for changing roles. However, when we, as educators, unburden ourselves of the role of expert and embrace the role of learner, we don't fear failure. We see it as opportunities for growth. Even more beautiful is the shift in relationships between kids, peers, and the world when we are willing to learn from each other. In order to evolve, we need to collaboratively engage in an ongoing process of improvement and analysis to make the changes necessary to meet the needs of all learners.

## ADULT LEARNING THEORY

Interestingly enough, respecting the adult learner through personalizing professional learning is not a new concept. In fact, Malcolm Knowles, a pioneer and expert on *andragogy,* the art and science of adult learning, provided the Four Principles of Andragogy in 1984b:

1. Adults need to be involved in the planning and evaluation of their instruction.
2. Experience (including mistakes) provides the basis for the learning activities.
3. Adults are most interested in learning subjects that have immediate relevance and impact to their job or personal life.
4. Adult learning is problem-centered rather than content-oriented. (Kearsley, 2010)

Building on these principles, we can leverage innovative, effective, and sustainable approaches to give all learners choice over time, place, path, and pace, and we are no longer bound to a one-size-fits-all approach to professional growth. We instead focus on learning relationships in a cycle of inquiry for professional learning.

## CYCLES OF INQUIRY FOR PROFESSIONAL LEARNING

What do we mean by "cycles of inquiry for professional learning"? In its most basic form, we find a *focus* that is impactful for our kids as well as the right grain size, we *learn* or unlearn and relearn in order to discover our best option(s), we *refine* as we implement that practice, and we constantly *reflect* on the impact to keep us moving toward success. This is an ongoing, iterative process.

As we researched for this book, we analyzed a number of cycles of inquiry—the 5 E's, ADDIE, Impact Cycle, and Learning Forward's Continuous Cycle of Improvement, just to name a few. We found that, to some extent, they were all the same and they were all different. As part of our learning process, we decided to create our own cycle of inquiry to capture the essential pieces, which we have named Focus, Learn, Refine, and Reflect. To be clear, our cycle of inquiry is *intentionally* generic. We are not trying to create a new model; rather, we are trying to be very clear that this is about reflective practice. To make connections to more specific cycles of inquiry, we added the action words from the other models we analyzed (see image below). We realized that we needed different words for different contexts. For example, a cycle of inquiry for learners in my class doesn't necessarily look like the cycle of inquiry I would use to improve my practice, but we are all engaged in cycles of inquiry. Again, below is our intentionally generic *Evolving Learner Cycle of Inquiry*. We will revisit it throughout the book, and we hope you find it helpful.

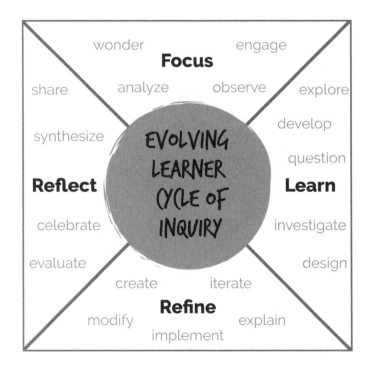

# ORGANIZATION OF THE BOOK

This book focuses on three main types of relationships for learning: learning from kids, learning from peers, and learning from the world. The order of this book is intentional. We start with learning from kids because we believe all thinking about teaching and learning should start with kids in mind. However, this book does not need to be read sequentially, making it accessible to even the busiest educator.

Within each chapter, we have carefully selected a few best practices to illustrate how intertwined the cycles of inquiry are for both kids and adult learners. We understand that you may want more information on certain topics, so the end of each chapter has a "Learn More" section that provides a deep dive into topics. Each chapter also ends with a review of tips as well as a "Thoughts, JOTs [Just One Thing], and Next Steps" workspace to capture your thinking. Plus, we will always share even more at evolvinglearning.org.

## Learning From Kids

> "None of us is as smart as all of us."
>
> —Ken Blanchard

This is a book about relationships for learning through a cycle of inquiry. It's about developing relationships with educators around the world to stretch our thinking. It's about developing relationships with peers and mentors to refine our practice. And it's also about developing relationships with kids, the most precious, abundant, and underutilized resource in virtually every classroom.

There is an assumption in any classroom that the teacher is there to add value by educating. The teacher has knowledge and techniques for taking kids to the next level. Conventional wisdom says, "If we put one of these skilled adults in a room with a group of kids, the teacher will make everyone smarter." Sadly, these assumptions do not usually carry over to the other people in the room: the kids. We believe this is a mistake. Drawing kids in as owners of the learning, rather than passive observers in their own education, helps boost engagement, creativity, and collaboration, which leads to deeper learning.

> **DRAWING KIDS IN AS OWNERS OF THE LEARNING, RATHER THAN PASSIVE OBSERVERS IN THEIR OWN EDUCATION, HELPS BOOST ENGAGEMENT, CREATIVITY, AND COLLABORATION, WHICH LEADS TO DEEPER LEARNING.**

To be clear, there is no substitute for a teacher's knowledge, experience, and techniques. Teachers are highly trained professionals employed to help educate. However, *how* those kids are educated is a constantly evolving combination of art and science. Simply put, we believe that traditional education is woefully underutilizing the unique perspectives and creativity that kids bring to classrooms and learning. Kids are the most abundant resource in our schools, and they are critical to personalizing learning for teachers.

In this section, we focus on two themes: (1) making thinking transparent to tailor instruction and promote teacher inquiry and (2) empowering ownership of learning for all. The focus on making thinking transparent is imperative to tailor instruction and promote teacher inquiry. This section of the book offers practical strategies for building community and giving every learner a voice while empowering the teacher to make informed instructional decisions. We also need to make thinking transparent in order to measure success in our own cycle of inquiry. Evolving to learn from kids, like the other sections of this book, is based in honoring the learner.

When we talk about "ownership of learning," we are talking about a shift from students who consume content to learners who create content through inquiry-based learning. The use of the words "students" and "learners" in the previous sentence was intentional. *Student* is a role and, often, it indicates a person's place in the classroom. In many ways, it is about a hierarchy of knowledge, experience, age, and so forth. However, at the root of *learner* is the verb *learn,* and the term could and should apply as much to the teacher as the child. We are not suggesting that the word *student* be removed from our vernacular. It isn't the word itself that is negative. What is important is that we thoughtfully redesign learning experiences to empower all learners (kids and adults) through learner-driven activities, projects, and collaboration. Furthermore, we need to rethink how we see pedagogical strategies and teacher practices to fully appreciate what is happening in inquiry-based learning environments with agency for all learners, both kids *and* adults.

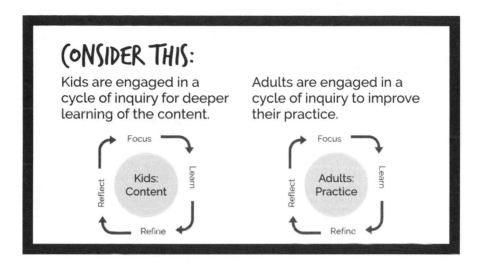

## CONSIDER THIS:

Kids are engaged in a cycle of inquiry for deeper learning of the content.

Adults are engaged in a cycle of inquiry to improve their practice.

Focus — Learn — Refine — Reflect

**Kids: Content**

Focus — Learn — Refine — Reflect

**Adults: Practice**

## Learning From Peers

"The only mistake you can make is not asking for help."
—Sandeep Jauhar

Think of one of the worst PDs that you have ever attended. Now think about what made it so bad. Was it the "sit and get" format? Was it an externally driven, one-size-fits-all PD session that you had no say in? If you answered yes to one or both of those questions, chances are that you did not feel like you were respected as a learner.

"Learning From Peers" is a chapter filled with proven strategies to create a culture of sharing and learning. There is tremendous power in learning from peers, and according to the Learning Forward standards, most professional learning should be job-embedded.

teachers

are

also

students

Imagine a first-year teacher who is unsure of how to implement district curriculum. We have all been there. Asking for support can be humbling and difficult. Asking for support as a veteran teacher can be humbling at a whole other level. As educators, we need to rid ourselves of the fear of admitting we are unsure about something. Our kids need their learning environment to be a safe space to ask for help and, similarly, educators need a safe space to ask for help that is job-embedded.

> **AS EDUCATORS, WE NEED TO RID OURSELVES OF THE FEAR OF ADMITTING WE ARE UNSURE ABOUT SOMETHING. OUR KIDS NEED THEIR LEARNING ENVIRONMENT TO BE A SAFE SPACE TO ASK FOR HELP AND, SIMILARLY, EDUCATORS NEED A SAFE SPACE TO ASK FOR HELP THAT IS JOB-EMBEDDED.**

Learning from peers is about tapping into strengths, building capacity, and empowering those around us on a daily basis. One way this can happen, and is happening, is through professional learning communities (PLCs) or instructional coaching. PLCs and coaching are inquiry-based and come in different forms, whether it be teacher teams or an onsite instructional coach. We will explore the different models through the work of leading experts and share innovative examples from practitioners in the field.

Relationships are key when it comes to coaching, and that is why everyone is involved—the administrator, coaches, teachers—*everyone.* Even coaches need coaching. Having someone invest in us, encourage us, and create a space for us to ask questions about our practice makes sense logically, and yet it is something that can be hard for us, as educators, to do. For educators, being vulnerable is a learned skill. Admitting to our peers, and to each other, that we can and *want to* learn from one another is one way we can evolve as learners.

## Learning From the World

As an educator or leader in education, a traditional job role is to *have answers.* Kids and colleagues depend on us for information, direction, and explanation. This is the epitome of the well-known idea of the "sage on the stage," or someone who *only* pontificates at the front of the room or from a place of power. This view of educators is now outdated and insufficient because learning is social, and learners need opportunities to collaborate, talk, research, and explore to achieve deeper learning. We now have opportunities to empower learners to own their own learning. In fact, according to the (Blackboard & Project Tomorrow) 2017 *Trends in Digital Learning* report,

> Teachers in blended learning classrooms are setting a new bar for transforming learning using technology. For example, 68% report that with the use of technology in their classroom they are better able to differentiate instruction for their students. (n.p.)

Furthermore, the findings indicate that,

> Teachers who have experienced online and blended classes for their own professional learning demonstrate advanced uses of technology with their own students, have stronger valuations on the role of technology within learning, and higher aspirations for leveraging technology to support transformed learning environments. (n.p.)

That is why it can be so frustrating and perplexing to see that teachers still experience professional development in a top-down, antiquated model that directly opposes the learning models that we want for our kids. Professional development, in fact, is something that *happens* to teachers, rather than something that educators actively pursue based on interest or the needs of their learners.

> "Everyone you will ever meet knows something you don't."
> —Bill Nye

Technology has changed the world in incredible ways, and that, in turn, should transform education and learning. Educators are helping to develop the future workforce and individuals who will help run, fix, operate, and build the technologies of tomorrow in roles that have yet to even be invented. However, the educational system and the way that teachers are developed and trained have changed very little. The good news is that we do not need to *wait* for a complete systemic change in order to significantly alter the way we run schools and classrooms. We all have the opportunity to be inquiry-driven, constantly learning from kids, peers, and the world around us.

> **WE DO NOT NEED TO *WAIT* FOR A COMPLETE SYSTEMIC CHANGE IN ORDER TO SIGNIFICANTLY ALTER THE WAY WE RUN SCHOOLS AND CLASSROOMS. WE ALL HAVE THE OPPORTUNITY TO BE INQUIRY-DRIVEN, CONSTANTLY LEARNING FROM KIDS, PEERS, AND THE WORLD.**

In fact, learning from the world has never been more accessible. The most current research, theories, data, and opinions on education, learning, teaching, and thinking are often just a click away. However (to paraphrase Mitchell Kapor in Chapter 3), this can often be like taking a drink from the educational fire hose. Where do we start? How can we make it more manageable and accessible? And how can we determine what is credible and worth our time? This chapter includes innovative approaches for making this task less daunting. With some key strategies and tools, learning from the world can be simple and straightforward, and it can take you in a completely unexpected direction, inspiring you and having a profound impact on your practice.

## OUR NOTE TO THE READER

As we started on this journey, we kept in mind that there is no "recipe" for professional learning. How could professional learning follow a recipe *and* be personalized? To be clear, the best practices that we share in each chapter are carefully curated, but they are not the only effective practices out there. After all, *equifinality* is absolutely a reality in education. Merriam-Webster defines equifinality as the property of allowing or having the same effect or result from different events. There are a number of successful districts, schools, and learners in the world, but these districts, schools, and learners are not doing the exact same thing. There simply isn't a one-size-fits-all way to be successful in teaching and learning for adults or kids. Rather, it is a combination of art and science that varies based on unique needs. That said, we are confident that within your own cycle of inquiry, the research-based strategies and examples that we share can be adapted to serve you in your unique situation.

# EQUIFINALITY

/equi finality/

: the property of allowing or having the same effect or result from different events

*Source:* "equifinality." Merriam-Webster.com/ 2019. https://www.meriam-webster.com (10 September 2019).

Thus far, we have been very explicit in introducing key elements for designing innovative, effective, and sustainable professional learning: adult learning theory, cycles of inquiry, and learning relationships. Since learning relationships are such a critical element in the successful models we will be sharing, we would be remiss if we didn't point out one more theme that runs throughout this book, social-emotional learning (SEL). The Collaborative for Academic, Social, and Emotional Learning (CASEL, 2019) website defines social-emotional learning as "the process through which children and adults understand and manage emotions, set and achieve positive goals, feel and show empathy for others, establish and maintain positive relationships, and make responsible decisions."

We love that this definition clearly articulates the connection between achievement and SEL. Unfortunately, far too often we find arbitrary separation of achievement and SEL, as if SEL is an unrelated, separate subject that we will teach once we are finished with the core subjects (if there is time) and has no direct correlation to learning. We believe that SEL is an essential piece that is ongoing in the learning culture, and you will find that it is a constant throughout this text. Sometimes we will label it explicitly, but often it is just a natural part of learning relationships in a cycle of inquiry.

Our hope for this book is that, as we share what is working for others, you are inspired to take pieces and adapt them to meet your needs and the needs of your peers. After all, regardless of your role in education, we are all advocates for learners. Please join us along the way as we discover how to evolve as learners and shift from traditional PD to personalized professional learning!

## THOUGHTS, JOTS, AND NEXT STEPS

# CHAPTER 1

LEARNING FROM KIDS

is about
**honoring the learner**

and leveraging the most abundant resource in our schools

## KIDS

### WHAT ARE THEY THINKING?
Making Thinking Transparent to Tailor
Instruction and Promote Teacher Inquiry

### OWNERSHIP OF LEARNING FOR ALL:
Shifting From Students Who Consume
Content to Learners Who Create Content

### CYCLES OF INQUIRY FOR KIDS AND ADULTS

### SPECTRUM FOR OWNERSHIP OF LEARNING

Instructional Practices That
Tailor Instruction and Promote
Teacher Inquiry

Instructional Practices That
Empower Learners

# HONOR THE LEARNER: KIDS

> "As children, we have a tenuous idea of love; we often try to quantify it with how much we feel seen and heard."
>
> —Adora Svitak, age 14

Imagine someone who has never experienced formal education walking into a traditional classroom for the very first time. The individual would probably notice that there is one person in the room who is working much harder than everyone else: the teacher. Why is that? There was a time when transferring knowledge was key, when books were rare and information was hard to access. Then came the printing press and eventually mass-produced textbooks. Arguably, the textbook could have been very disruptive, but in actuality, not much has changed. The focus was, and has remained in the vast majority of classrooms, on one person in front of the room disseminating information. Consider the graphic that follows, inspired by a question that Alan November often asks educators, "Who works the hardest in your classroom?"

This top-down approach is not new or unique to education; it has been practiced in all sectors, from factories and companies to the military. The reality is that society and the way we live evolves and, to stay relevant, education needs to evolve too. One way to think about this shift is the concept of "genius" versus "scenius." The term *scenius* originates from Brian Eno, a musician and producer, and we came to know this term via Austin Kleon (2017) who says, "To put it even more simply: Genius is an *egosystem*, scenius is an *ecosystem*."

# WHO IS WORKING THE HARDEST IN THIS CLASSROOM?

Teacher

Students

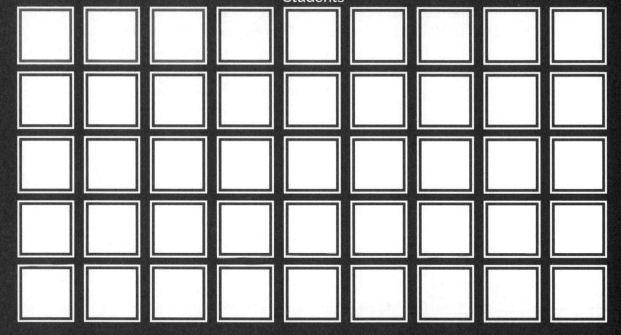

The big idea here is that we value the gifts of individuals, and we collaborate to take the gifts of individuals much further. To put it in the context of learning from kids, teachers are unique individuals with their own unique gifts (knowledge, skills, and dispositions), and kids are also unique individuals with their own such gifts. To leverage both, we need to shift from teacher driven to learner driven, and when we say learner, we are talking about the kids *and* the adults.

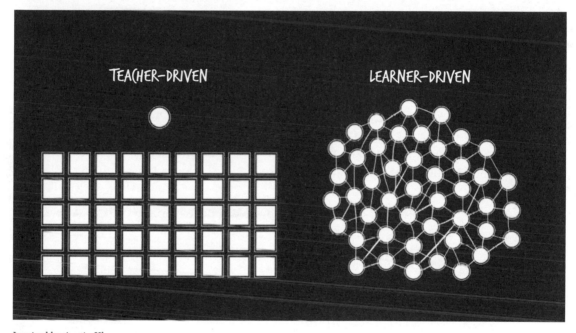

Inspired by Austin Kleon

Looking at the teacher-driven versus learner-driven visual, which system promotes the most engagement, for both kid and adult learners? The data on the importance of engagement is clear, and decades worth of surveys and analysis by Gallup's research team reveals some basic truths. For example, of the 47% of students who say they are engaged in school, those students are 2.5 times more likely to get good grades and do well in school. They are also "4.5 times more likely to be hopeful about the future than their actively disengaged peers"

(Hodges, 2018). Engagement is increased and learning is optimized when everyone contributes in a scenius ecosystem.

The key to scenius for learning is that kids and adults are simultaneously engaged in cycles of inquiry. Revisiting the graphic below, consider this: Kids are engaged in a cycle of inquiry for deeper learning of the content. Adults are engaged in a cycle of inquiry to improve their practice. We believe that both are critical, and we question how often they are practiced in harmony. Moreover, when they are practiced in harmony, are we even aware of it? Most educators have engaged in a cycle of inquiry regarding their practice, whether it was intentional or not. The reality is that professional learning takes place in practices that we don't typically think of as professional learning, but it *is* professional learning and we need to be intentional about it to be as efficient and effective as possible. That is what this chapter on learning from kids is about. We want to highlight practices that are already happening in classrooms to create deeper learning, and we want to talk about being intentional with the professional learning opportunities that are presented to us each and every day that we work with kids.

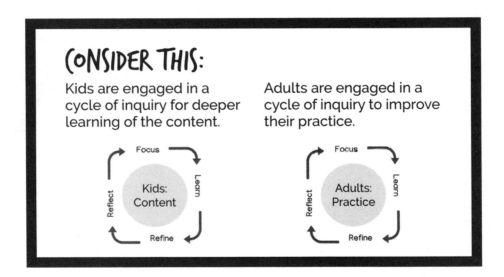

The idea of learning from kids could elicit very different responses from educators. For some, the concept is a core value already implemented in their practice. For others, it may challenge deeply entrenched beliefs about the role of adults and children as well as bring up concerns around valuing the institution of education. It is not our intention to insert a value judgment here. Our years of experience have taught us the importance of honoring the tried-and-true practices as well as the master teachers who can engage a group of kids in a traditional lecture without any props or devices. However, if we can all agree that our primary responsibility is to our learners and that they are in fact our clientele, can we also agree that we must respect our clients' ideas, experiences, and perspective to serve them better? With that in mind, what would it mean to think of our kids as the ultimate human resource, the ultimate opportunity for professional learning? Though it might strike some educators as a huge paradigm shift, professional learning is often happening when you don't even realize it. We need to value our kids as a resource for teaching and learning.

> **IF WE CAN ALL AGREE THAT OUR PRIMARY RESPONSIBILITY IS TO OUR LEARNERS AND THAT THEY ARE IN FACT OUR CLIENTELE, CAN WE ALSO AGREE THAT WE MUST RESPECT OUR CLIENTS' IDEAS, EXPERIENCES, AND PERSPECTIVE TO SERVE THEM BETTER?**

Learning Forward's Standards for Professional Learning urge us to prioritize human, fiscal, material, technology, and time resources. When we truly value our kids and all they have to offer as a resource, the math makes another compelling argument for learning from kids. The *Education at a Glance 2015* report by the Organization for Economic Cooperation and Development (OECD) found that U.S. educators for lower elementary or middle school spend an average of 981 hours in the classroom per year (OECD.org). For most of the United States, there is a required minimum of 180 school days. Compare that to the amount of time teachers spend on professional learning. A report published by The New Teacher Project (TNTP, 2015) surveyed educators and found that less than 10% of their time is spent in professional learning activities. That may seem like a good amount of time, but according to *Professional Learning in the Learning Profession: A Status Report on Teacher Development in the United States and Abroad* (Wei, Darling-Hammond, Andree, Richardson, & Orphanos, 2009),

> Other nations that outperform the United States on international assessments invest heavily in professional learning and build time

for ongoing, sustained teacher development and collaboration into teachers' work hours. American teachers spend much more time teaching and have significantly less time to plan and learn together, and to develop high-quality curriculum and instruction than teachers in other nations. (p. 6)

*Source:* unsplash.com/@tcrawlers

The reality is that when teachers do get professional learning time, it is often right before a new school year is about to start, which is a very stressful time, or at the end of the school year when teachers need a break and are possibly burnt out. Furthermore, given the limited amount of time for traditional PD, we sometimes see an overcorrection or possibly even a hyper-overcorrection where a day of professional learning is extended: Instead of doing a workshop for 4–6 hours, let's make it 8 hours to get the most bang for our buck. However, asking educators to attempt to absorb more content (outside of a job-embedded context) when they passed their maximum cognitive load hours ago is futile and, worse, counterproductive. We need time to process, plan, and test new knowledge. Overloading the human brain even more doesn't help. If anything, it ensures that nothing new will be put into practice, since we all know that it is highly unlikely you will spend the 8 hours in the workshop and then go straight into implementation. More typically, teachers leave the workshop with piles of notes and to-do lists, their heads spinning, only to get overwhelmed or strapped for time and abandoning them Monday morning.

While the ongoing accessibility to learners and the idea of maximizing resources are certainly key parts of learning from kids, they are by no means the motivator. The motivator is that we believe that kids bring unique perspectives and creativity that can be harnessed to improve learning for all. We also believe in the work of John Hattie and other education thought leaders who advocate for learning through the eyes of kids. In doing so, we help learners become their own teachers while we improve our practice. Kids truly are the most precious, abundant, and underutilized resource in every classroom. They are also critical to personalizing learning for teachers. We often hear about the one-size-fits-all workshop and the need to personalize. There is no better way to personalize learning than staying focused on your kids and learning from them.

**KIDS TRULY ARE THE MOST PRECIOUS, ABUNDANT, AND UNDERUTILIZED RESOURCE IN EVERY CLASSROOM. THEY ARE ALSO CRITICAL TO PERSONALIZING LEARNING FOR TEACHERS.**

# LEVERAGING THE MOST ABUNDANT RESOURCES IN OUR SCHOOLS

This chapter on learning from kids is really about a mindset. Being willing to learn from experts and peers is one thing, but are you willing to learn from kids? This sounds like a simple question, but for many of us this can really challenge our egos as well as a traditional approach to education that is deeply ingrained in us because it is the system in which the vast majority of us grew up. Did you enjoy school? Were you good at it? Did you like the teacher being in control? Or did you prefer it when you had choices that leveraged your special talents?

Given the virtually ubiquitous access to the internet and social media, the youth of America have more opportunities than any other previous generation to have their voices heard, and we find it rather remarkable that we don't hear more about learning from kids. It's possible that it is too big a paradigm shift. It's possible that we underestimate the ability of our youth. Could it be both? In her 2010 TED Talk, Adora Svitak (age 12 at the time) advocated that, "Learning between grown-ups and kids should be reciprocal," and she called on us to trust kids and expect more from them. At the time of this writing, her TED Talk has over 5.5 million views! Clearly, we are not the only ones who agree with Adora. So, how do we do what she says? Well, there isn't just one way to do it. The beauty of learning from kids is that it is incredibly personalized, and there are many different ways this professional learning can take form.

We recently interviewed Adora, now 20 years old at the time of this writing, and asked her what inspired her to advocate for learning from kids.

*Growing up, did you have experiences where learning truly was reciprocal between the adults and kids?*

My parents tried hard to model a lot of reciprocal learning, and to emphasize to my sister Adrianna and me (see photo) that learning didn't just happen in one direction. To that end,

I had a lot of opportunities to teach others. I had a younger neighbor who was just learning how to read, and my mom encouraged me to help teach him phonics. There are cute photos of us sitting by a chalkboard together. When my mom, sister, and I would go on walks to the local park, one of my favorite habits was to jump up on top of a big rock and give impromptu speeches. My house was never a "children should be seen and not heard" kind of house; my parents encouraged us to air our opinions and defend them, even—maybe, especially—when we disagreed with them. That's how Adrianna and I ended up drafting a document we called the "Declaration of Independence From the Groans" ("groans" was our derisive term for grown-ups, which I guess as a seven-year-old I didn't have the fore-

*Source:* Adora Svitak

sight to imagine I would ever grow to regret. Hindsight is 20/20!) In our Declaration, we expressed our strong belief in youth self-determination and not letting adults get in the way of having fun. I love that we did that because it reflects just how free we felt to say whatever we believed.

On a more practical note, I also learned pretty early on that my parents still had opportunities to learn. Many children with an immigrant parent can probably relate to this experience. I grew up proofreading my mom's emails for her, looking for grammatical idiosyncrasies, poring over sentences to find a misplaced modifier here or comma splice there. English wasn't my mom's first language, but it was mine, and so there were corrections I knew how to make but didn't know how to explain. "That's just the way it is," I'd sometimes say, before realizing that that answer wasn't good enough. In this situation, I played the role of being the teacher, or at least the editor. I actually learned a lot about grammar from my mom. After all, it was only in the face of her demand for a rule or an explanation that I conducted additional research to try to understand.

What keeps a lot of parents from developing environments of reciprocal learning is fear—fear that when your kids realize you don't know everything, they might not respect you. Fear that you'll look stupid. I grew up with parents who treated me like I had something important to contribute, so I've never known anything different. I can assure you that now, having seen families where kids are not treated that way, I wouldn't have changed a thing. I respect my parents so much more for being upfront about the areas where they can learn from others of any age.

*What advice would you give to educators who are ready to learn from kids?*

I'd recommend that if you haven't already, you practice having informal conversations with kids in small groups about important issues. It might surprise you how full of opinions kids can be. Try asking kids about friendship, beauty, happiness, or love. Notice the things they observe and the things that seem inexplicable to them. Sometimes there is as much to be learned from what's *not* said as what *is*. What are the things they *don't* care about?

I'd also recommend that you try to extend the lessons you learn past just the moment when you're sitting with kids and having a conversation. Think about applying them in other areas of your life. How can the boundless creativity of a fourth grader experimenting with finger paints inspire creativity in your practice? How can the merciless honesty of a kindergartener make you think about how you relate to, and what you demand from, those in power? Just like adults, kids want to see a world where their words can have an impact. By showing them that what they've said has impacted you, you're teaching them a powerful lesson about their own agency.

Adora was very fortunate to grow up in a loving home where she always felt valued. Not all of our kids experience that kind of home life. As educators, we can engage with families and encourage them to value their kids and their gifts that we see in school, but the reality is that we ultimately don't have control over how valued our kids feel at home. We can, however, make sure they feel valued in the precious hours they are in our care.

So how do our kids feel at school? In a joint initiative between the Yale Center for Emotional Intelligence and the Born This Way Foundation, the Emotion Revolution study asked over 22,000 middle and high school students across the United States "How do you feel each day in school?" The top three responses were *tired, bored,* and *stressed.* Revisiting 14-year-old Adora's quote, "As children, we have a tenuous idea of love; we often try to quantify it with how much we feel seen and heard," and considering the traditional model of education, it is hard to miss the likely correlation. Is it possible that kids are feeling tired, bored, and stressed in school because they don't feel seen and heard? Is it possible that empowering kids by making learning truly reciprocal between adults and kids could help solve this problem? We believe the answer is yes.

## IS IT POSSIBLE THAT KIDS ARE FEELING TIRED, BORED, AND STRESSED IN SCHOOL BECAUSE THEY DON'T FEEL SEEN AND HEARD?

Moving forward, we will focus on two themes in this chapter as we explore how educators are learning from kids: (1) making thinking transparent to tailor instruction and promote teacher inquiry, and (2) empowering ownership of learning for all. Please note that the two themes are not mutually exclusive. Please also note that as we share strategies and examples of learning from kids, the line between adult learning and kid learning will frequently get blurred. As previously discussed, these are in fact two different layers, two different cycles of inquiry, but often there are so intertwined, it is hard to tease the two apart. We are okay with that, and we hope that you are too.

# WHAT ARE THEY THINKING? MAKING THINKING TRANSPARENT TO TAILOR INSTRUCTION AND PROMOTE TEACHER INQUIRY

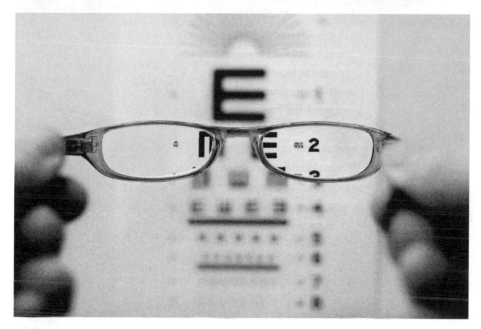

*Source:* unsplash.com/@dtravisphd

As a teacher, you may have gazed out among your learners and wondered, "What are they thinking?" Perhaps this has happened to you on more than one occasion. It is really interesting to consider the dynamics of a classroom when there is one of you and so many of them, in most cases, 20 to 30 or more of them. You might think, how can I possibly manage this? How do I ask a question and see every learner's answer? How do I empower them to ask questions? How do I quantify the success of my teaching? How do I adjust my instructional moves throughout a lesson to meet the needs of my learners? How do I hone my practice based on what I see and learn? Many of these questions refer to formative assessment, and we now have the strategies and tools to accomplish these things.

# ONE OF ME & SO MANY OF THEM

How can I possibly manage?
How do I ask a question and see every learner's answer?
How do I empower them to ask questions?
How do I use data to adjust my instructional moves in real time?
How do I quantify the success of my teaching?
How do I hone my practice based on what I see and learn?

We know that we need assessments that are formative. That is, we need assessments that allow us to analyze the data and, based on what we learn, to design, implement, and evaluate learning experiences. This cycle of inquiry guides instruction and informs our practice. This is learning design *and* this is professional learning!

Strategies and tools to help us see what kids are thinking are not new. We have had pencil and paper, individual whiteboards, and so on. However, in the landscape of educational technology, there has been an explosion of apps and services that empower teachers to "see" what kids are thinking in real time by capturing their ideas as well as answers to both open- and closed-ended questions. These tools cover a wide range of options, including, but not limited to, response systems that capture multiple-choice responses from learners and instantaneously create graphs and charts quantifying effectiveness of instruction and informing decisions in the actual moment of instruction.

We also have apps that allow a teacher to ask an open-ended question and provide space for every single learner to simultaneously share ideas. We even have tools that aggregate those responses to create *word clouds*, a visual representation in which the more a specific word is used by the learners, the larger it appears. These word clouds can be used to analyze themes in learner responses. Consider this: How often have you, in your role as a teacher, asked a question to a room full of students and the same three or four students raise their hand to answer every single time. What is happening with other learners in the room? Are all of them disengaged? Or, is it possible that at least some of them are thinking critically and processing to formulate a truly thoughtful response that reflects empathy and understanding. When do those learners get an opportunity to contribute? When do they get the time and space to share their thinking? When we leverage these powerful resources, not only do we honor those who are truly listening and thinking, but we are also truly listening and thinking in return.

To be clear, the tool often gets all of the attention, but it is critical that the learning design is first and foremost grounded in research-based instructional strategies. The tools available now are so much more sophisticated that the impact is much greater on instruction and professional learning, when there is sound pedagogy driving their use. Therefore, we must start with the learning goals, not the tool. As instructional designers, we are intentional in developing inquiry-based activities that deepen learning, and we are intentional in how we gather data (qualitative and quantitative) about our learners to guide us in our own cycle of inquiry. We need to think critically about the type of content we're working with and match accordingly. In other words, if I'm asking learners a high-level question, I need to give them more processing time rather than rush to get an answer from the first few kids who raise their hand. I want all learners to think about the question from different perspectives and apply empathy.

For example, if we are beginning to learn about a new topic, I want to engage my learners, and I also need to know what their prior knowledge is, so my goal is to capture open-ended responses. However, I also want a quick way to aggregate their ideas so we can discuss as a class. Based on that instructional goal, I choose to have learners generate a word cloud. My first step is to ask learners to go online to the word cloud service I'm currently using. (These free services come and go, so it isn't worth referencing a specific tool, but in Chapter 3 on *learning from the world,* we will talk about how you can find what you need, when you need it!) Then I ask them to type as many words as they can think of that are related to our topic. Once everyone has submitted their words, I reveal the word cloud and ask learners to discuss. If our topic was Relationship Skills and Social Awareness, results from our word cloud might look like this:

The size of each word reflects frequency, so we observe which words are large (submitted most) and which words are small (submitted least), and we analyze, looking for patterns. I ask the group, "Looking at our word cloud, what knowledge is already in the room? Where do we need to focus our learning?" This is the beginning of *their* inquiry cycle, and it is also the beginning of *my* inquiry cycle. As part of my inquiry cycle, I'm also analyzing the results of the word cloud to see what is missing and, equally important, I'm seeing the topic through the eyes of kids. What do they think is important?

Please note: In the subsequent chapters on *learning from peers* and *learning from the world,* we will explore specific ways to build learning relationships and expand your community, bringing "peers" and the "world" into your cycle of inquiry for professional learning. For example, the word cloud that my class created is data that I can take to my "peers" for further analysis. In addition, based on our analysis, we can reach out to the "world" and ask for additional ideas in planning next steps in our cycle of inquiry.

The beauty of these learning relationships with kids, peers, and the world is that our cycle of inquiry involves many different perspectives and we avoid *solutionitis.* We came to know this term from the book *Learning to Improve: How America's Schools Can Get Better* by Bryk, Gomez, Grunow, and LeMahieu (2016).

> Solutionitis is the propensity to jump quickly on a solution before fully understanding the exact problem to be solved. It is a form of groupthink in which a set of shared beliefs result in an incomplete analysis of the problem to be addressed and fuller consideration of potential problem-solving alternatives. When decision makers see complex matters through a narrow lens, solutionitis lures them into unproductive strategies. (p. 24)

Solutionitis is the enemy of a true cycle of inquiry for both kids and adults. In a kid learner's cycle of inquiry, solutionitis is a barrier to deeper learning. In an adult learner's cycle of inquiry, solutionitis is a barrier to improvement in practice.

## Cycles of Inquiry for Kids and Adults

Before grade school, kids ask an average of over 300 questions a day (according to a study by Littlewoods.com). At the time of this writing, all three of the authors of this book are mothers to preschoolers, so we can attest to the constant barrage of questions! How many questions a day do you think kids ask after starting elementary school? How many do you think a kindergartener asks compared to a fourth grader, compared to an eighth grader, and compared to a twelfth grader? We have asked educators and parents around the world this question, and the overwhelming majority agree that the number of questions kids ask decreases over time as they progress through grades, especially by the time kids reach upper elementary. The traditional approach to education simply doesn't have room for kids to ask lots of questions. In fact, it discourages it. Can you recall a time when you were a learner and were asked to "save your questions till the end"? Obviously, it would be distracting (and possibly rude) if there was constant questioning during a lecture, but if a child is struggling and has to wait until the end of a lesson to get answers, how will he or she be successful? It's no wonder that the three of us are fans of the 5 E's instructional model.

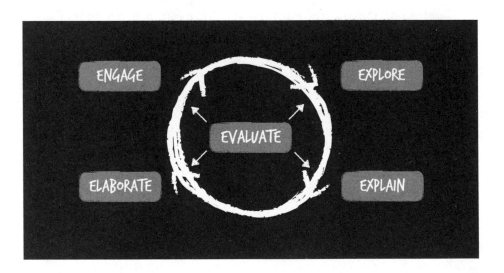

Consider the order of the 5 E's, as shown in the image: Engage, Explore, Explain, and Elaborate, with Evaluate as a constant throughout. Also, note that Engage and Explore are intentionally placed before Explain. In a traditional lesson, "explain," or direct instruction, happens at the beginning of a lesson. As you may have noticed, the example of using the word cloud to activate prior knowledge (shared previously in this section) would be considered an "engage" activity in a 5 E's lesson. Using an inquiry-based approach to learning design creates a shift, moving the focus from direct instruction (teacher-focused) and providing opportunities to leverage the inquisitive nature of kids while empowering them as learners. It also empowers the teacher to be present in watching, listening to, and learning from kids so that the adult learner is also involved in inquiry-based learning as a professional!

The 5 E's constructivist model of learning encourages questioning early on during the "engage" or "explore" phase to allow the learner to build on prior knowledge/experiences and make connections. The "explain" portion of the lesson then addresses unanswered questions, but it is critical to keep in mind that, in inquiry-based learning cycles, we often move back and forth between steps, as learning is messy and rarely fits into a perfectly linear process. Throughout a 5 E's learning experience, there are many ways to make thinking transparent and then tailor instruction. In this next section, we will explore stories from educators as well as very specific strategies to achieve this. As we share these stories and strategies, we encourage you to focus not only on the learning gains, but also on how teachers are empowered to hone their professional practice through a cycle of inquiry.

Furthermore, as you focus on an educator's cycle of inquiry in the examples that follow, remember that the cycle of inquiry must be continuous and must include *kids*, *peers*, and *the world*. Learning Forward's *cycle of continuous improvement* illustrates how this looks at the school level working with peers and the world.

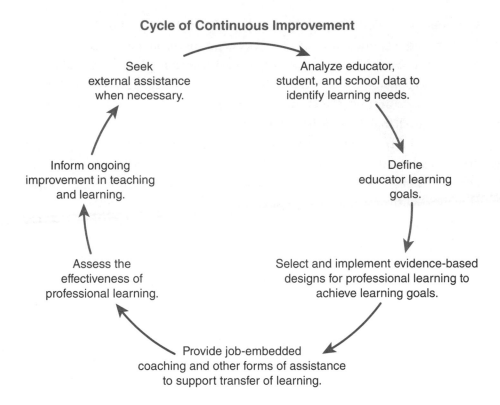

**Cycle of Continuous Improvement**

Seek external assistance when necessary.

Analyze educator, student, and school data to identify learning needs.

Define educator learning goals.

Select and implement evidence-based designs for professional learning to achieve learning goals.

Provide job-embedded coaching and other forms of assistance to support transfer of learning.

Assess the effectiveness of professional learning.

Inform ongoing improvement in teaching and learning.

*Source:* Learning Forward, "A Cycle of Continuous Improvement." Retrieved September 2019 from https://learningforward.org/docs/default-source/publicationssection/Transform/tool-cycle-of-continuous-improvement.pdf?sfvrsn=0

## Empower Learners to Ask Their Own Questions

I (Lainie) was recently working with a group of educators, and we were talking about the endless amount of online tools we now have access to that give us a variety of ways to do a quick check for understanding and make instructional decisions on the fly. One of the teachers shared that her learners were obsessed with an online tool that "gamified" formative assessment. Basically, learners respond to questions online using electronic devices, and points are awarded based on speed and accuracy. (Note: While these gamification tools can be controversial because some would argue that it isn't appropriate for all learners and the questions are often about recall, we find that when carefully implemented, these tools paired with solid pedagogy in a low-risk environment definitely have a place in providing motivation and engagement.) The teacher went on to admit that she doesn't know how to use this online tool to create any of the quizzes. Her learners create all of the quizzes! This is an example of leveraging the most valuable resource in the classroom. Not only did this teacher allow her learners to take ownership of the learning, but the process of developing the questions and answers was actually a much higher-level thinking activity than taking the quizzes themselves. These learners had to develop quality questions with the correct answers, distractors as well as other reasonable answer choices, and watching her learners develop these questions actually gave her more insight into their thinking than the results on the quizzes! Equally important to her professional learning, this teacher discovered that empowering her kids led to better results than if she had taken the lead in creating the formative assessments herself.

In the previous example, an online gamification tool motivated the kids to create questions, but there are other ways to inspire kids to develop questions. In the book *Make Just One Change: Teach Students to Ask Their Own Questions* by Dan Rothstein and Luz Santana (2014), the authors contend that "the single most essential skill for learning" is formulating one's own questions. The book, as well as the authors' nonprofit educational organization, the Right Question Institute (RQI), also provide what a growing number of educators find to be the simplest, most powerful strategy to teach that skill, the Question Formulation Technique (QFT).

Designing the question focus is the responsibility of the teacher (we encourage collaborating with *peers* and/or *the world* whenever possible). The teacher will need to pick a statement, image, graph, equation, piece of audio, object or title, and so forth from the curriculum content that will inspire learners to generate as many questions as possible. Kids take the lead on generating questions and, during this part of the process, one of the teacher's primary roles is to ensure that learners do not stop to answer, judge, or discuss the questions. This part is critical, especially when questions are being generated in a group. If there is judgment of anyone's questions (good or bad), we lose out on ideas. If someone says, "That's a terrible question," the learner who offered the question shuts down for fear of embarrassment, but equally detrimental to the brainstorming is when someone says, "That's a great question." When others in the group hear that positive feedback, they are less likely to contribute. After all, (in their minds) someone else already produced the best question. We have seen this happen with adults and kids. There should be no judgment while producing questions, period. With regard to professional learning and the teachers' cycle

# QUESTION FORMULATION TECHNIQUE (QFT) PROTOCOL

- Design a question focus
- Produce questions
- Work with closed-ended & open-ended questions
- Prioritize questions
- Plan next steps
- Reflect

of inquiry, it is important that teachers watch and listen to the questions that kids are asking. The questions generated are data that can be shared with peers and the world as we move forward in our own cycle of inquiry.

In the Australian practitioner vignette to follow, you will discover how this practice provides powerful insight that guides a teacher's professional learning. Note: After generating questions, the process focuses on the concept of closed-ended versus open-ended questions, followed by prioritizing the questions produced and planning next steps in learning. The final step, reflection, is critical. To learn more about QFT, visit rightquestion.org.

## LEARNING FROM KIDS IN ACTION: QUESTION FORMULATION TECHNIQUE (QFT)

**Melissa Marshall**
*Head of Digital Learning/Head of Technology and Commerce*
*Santa Maria College (school for girls ages 5–12)*
*Attadale, Western Australia*

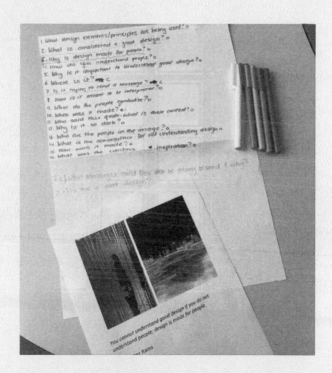

*(Continued)*

(Continued)

*How does using the Question Formulation Technique (QFT) help you improve your practice?*

One of the first things I do after we have completed the QFT is to collect student work and examine their questions. In the images included on the preceding page and below, the first image shows students just asking questions about the image and ignoring the quote. In the second image, students have taken the quote into context with the image. This tells me that the students might be far more interested in the image, or I need to make the goal of the activity a little more clear.

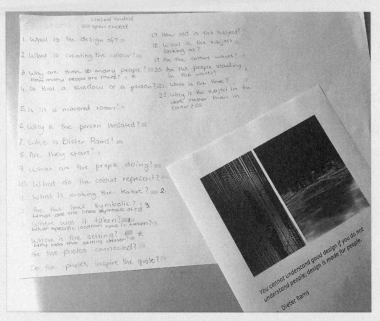

The number of open- versus closed-ended questions also gives me valuable information about what sorts of investigations the students are more prone to. In science, students tend to ask more open-ended questions, so we have focused on also valuing closed-ended questions to gain accurate data quickly. Many younger students have not been taught the difference between these question types, and once they learn them, they can then apply them to the sorts of questions that they want answers to.

This is also an important piece in my own professional learning. Listening to students' questions and examining their work is part of my own cycle of inquiry. The QFT process helps me uncover bias, or a misconception, or perhaps an area in which my teaching was lacking. If students are still confused on a topic, listening to their questions will help me figure out what is happening for them. I can also ask them questions or give them an open-ended activity to demonstrate understanding. Once I have these responses, I can sort them into groups based on lower, middle, and higher levels of understanding. Next lesson, I can pair up students with low and high levels of understanding for some peer coaching or a Socratic seminar, so that the higher levels can be modeled and discussed in the class and the thinking can be made more visible. This helps the higher-level students clarify their understanding, and the lower-level students now have a model to help them explain their own ideas.

Using the QFT ties directly back to what we discussed earlier when we posed the question, "Who is working hardest in the classroom?" Consider this: Who is asking the most questions in the classroom?

A common thread in all of the stories and strategies that we have shared and will continue to share is that educators are rethinking their role not only to improve instruction, but also to improve their own professional learning. It is about being inquiry-driven as an adult learner, and part of the challenge with that is that we need to *unlearn* how we teach. Consider the example of the teacher who didn't know how to use the online gamification tool. Someone in a traditional educator's mindset might say, "No, we won't be using this" or "We can't use this until I have been to a training on it." This teacher learned to empower her kids and in the process, the activity led to deeper learning. In the example of an educator using the QFT, or some other strategy to encourage learner-driven questioning, the teacher will need to "unlearn" being the person in the room who asks the majority of questions.

Using QFT, Melissa is able to uncover bias, misconceptions, and opportunities to improve her instruction. She is also able to take the learners' thinking, which is now transparent, and share it with her *peers* and *the world* to avoid solutionitis. Peers and the world can change our preconceived notions and offer us insight into how we move forward in our practice. However, please note: We are not advocating that teachers should never ask questions. We know that questioning is a highly effective instructional strategy that dates back to Socrates. In fact, teacher questioning is part of QFT, but it occurs at the end of a learning cycle, not at the beginning.

In our next research-based instructional practice, Peer Instruction, we explore a methodology based on teacher questioning throughout the learning process. Regardless of the strategy, the key point is that we need to unlearn our role so that we can make an objective decision choosing and implementing the pedagogy that provides our kids the best learning experiences while continuing to improve our practice.

## Peer Instruction (PI)

> "The fellow-pupil can help more than the master because he knows less. The difficulty we want him to explain is one he has recently met. The expert met it so long ago he has forgotten."
>
> —C. S. Lewis

This C. S. Lewis quote clearly illustrates a struggle that every educator has faced: the inability to understand how a learner doesn't understand what I, the teacher, am so clearly explaining! Dr. Eric Mazur, a Harvard University professor and a self-proclaimed "converted lecturer," realized his traditional lectures weren't working and developed *peer instruction (PI),* an interactive, research-based teaching method. PI solves this problem and reimagines the teacher's role by leveraging social learning and technology to help those who are struggling to grasp a concept, while empowering those who do understand to take a leadership role and deepen their own learning.

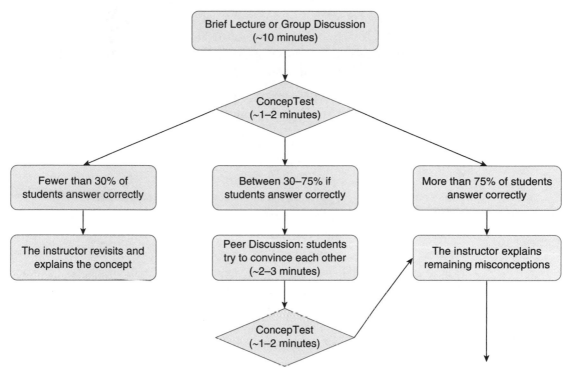

*Source:* Eric Mazur, *Peer Instruction: A User's Manual.* Pearson (1996).

The process is as follows:

- Teacher uses a digital response system to ask a question (ConcepTest) based on a mini-lecture, pre-class assignment, etc.
- Learners think about the answer.
- Learners commit to their individual answer (without talking to their peers).
- Teacher reviews responses and makes an on-the-fly instructional decision.
  - The vast majority of learners know this concept (greater than 75%), so I will move on to the next concept.
  - Very few learners understand this concept (less than 30%) so I need to find a completely new approach/way to explain.
  - There is enough knowledge in the room for peers to teach each other (30%–75% of students answered the ConcepTest correctly).
- During Peer Instruction, learners share their thinking and justify their answers to each other.

- Teacher uses the digital response system to re-ask the question (Concep-Test), and learners give their individual answer. Note: Learners are encouraged to change their answer if their peer convinced them that their previous response was incorrect.

- Teacher reviews the new responses and makes an instructional decision about further discussion of the concept or moving on to a new concept.

As an educator, circulating around the room and listening during the social learning component, it is an amazing opportunity to take in the transparent thinking! Not only do learners get a chance to learn from each other, but equally important, you get a chance to learn from the learners. It is truly fascinating to discover a new way to explain a concept and even more so when it is from the perspective of a child. As part of our own cycle of inquiry, we will also share these results and our learning with our *peers*, possibly in the form of professional learning communities (PLCs) and *the world* as part of our professional learning network (PLN). PLCs and PLNs can be incredibly powerful in our adult-learner cycle of inquiry and will be discussed in detail in Chapters 2 and 3 on learning from peers and learning from the world, respectively. To learn more about PI, visit peerinstruction.net or read the study at web.mit.edu/jbelcher/www/TEALref/Crouch_Mazur.pdf.

In the vignette that follows, Mrs. Megan Waddell Trimnal, a science teacher in North Carolina, shares her cycle of inquiry to improve her practice through the use of peer instruction. As she recounts her inquiry-based approach to implementing a new practice, note how reflective she is about her practice, how she is constantly evaluating and iterating as she learns. Please also note that both Megan and her learners are simultaneously engaged in a cycle of inquiry. Megan's cycle of inquiry is about her practice and the kids' cycle of inquiry is for content/skills.

## LEARNING FROM KIDS IN ACTION: PEER INSTRUCTION

### Mrs. Megan Waddell Trimnal
*Science Teacher*
*South Point High School, North Carolina*

After I was introduced to Mazur's peer instruction, I dove into this experiment and started using his techniques in my classroom. I had been around teenagers enough to know that they have a lot to say; have the ability to defend themselves; and would be more likely to listen to one another, rather than listening to me at the front of the room. Well, I was right, and of course, so was Mazur. I usually gave thirty-question unit tests with an opportunity to complete test corrections for their wrong answers. My students were not taking advantage of the test correction opportunity, and I was wasting time. I knew I needed to change my practice. So I gave a twenty-five–question test, and after everyone had completed it, I had students take the same test again with a partner. Students did not know what they missed on the individual test but had to work together on the second test. This certainly was not a waste of time. Instead of sitting quietly and "pretending" to complete corrections, my students were *actively engaged* in discussing the subject matter and having conversations as well as debates on answer choices—a glorious moment in this teacher's day. The test grade included the individual score as well as the partner score. It wasn't about the grade; it was about the process. I have used a slew of different protocols for "take the test twice," and each time I have those moments of sweetness as students grapple with the material. I realized that I was not the most important person in the room; *the students* have that role.

Up to that point, I had been so rigid in my classroom, with notes and labs and assessments. It was my way or the highway, and everything had to mimic my examples. Good thing my students knew I loved them and would do whatever I asked. It was a disservice to them; they were not learning to think for themselves. *I had greatly underestimated my students.* If students can learn from each other through peer instruction, they can also learn from themselves through self-assessment. My PLC designed a protocol to give short mini-assessments that were grouped by standards, and the feedback displayed what area that individual needed to study and readdress. Students *analyzed* their own work and *chose* an area to focus on. They were given *choices* of study delivery, including games, matching, writing, real world scenarios, interactives, etc. Another lesson: My students love choice. I gave them choices, and they gave attention and time. Again, another glorious moment. I now think of assessments completely differently. I use a variety of techniques including daily low-stakes quizzing and open-ended questions. I use a lot of sketches, drawings, word connections, and written summaries. There is no one size fits all. I use all of the sizes. Monotony is gone, students' work looks different from each other, and they are each learning to be learners—lifelong learners.

I was a lateral-entry teacher, a scientist first. I thought I had so much to offer, if they would only listen. I do have a lot to offer, but so do they! They deserve a teacher that allows them to take control of their own learning rather than feeding them lecture after lecture. I thought they needed intense structure and constant assessment. When I let go of the structure and started using assessments as learning tools for growth, I was able to see students that are curious, hardworking, and flourishing individually. For a long time, I was too afraid to experiment with assessments because I had a high-stakes state test at the end of the semester. I am so glad I took the leap to peer instruction, self-assessment, and alternative assessments; my test scores only grew, and my kids received the instruction they deserve.

Megan's inspirational story is an example of how making the shift to *scenius* and learning from and with kids leads to engaged learners and the ability to hone one's professional practice. Yes, her gradual release of responsibility through peer instruction, self-assessment, and alternative assessments all provided positive gains for her learners, but equally important is the professional learning she experienced through her inquiry-based approach to her own practice. Megan is constantly iterating to refine her professional skills through her cycle of inquiry that includes learning from kids, peers (PLCs), and the world (social media).

> "The smartest person in the room, is the room."
> —David Weinberger

If David Weinberger's famous quote is right, is it possible that the best teacher in the room, is the room? Peer Instruction, rethinking assessment protocols, and empowering kids to ask high-quality questions are just a few strategies that leverage the collective knowledge and perspectives in the room to make thinking transparent so as to tailor instruction and promote teacher inquiry. Moving forward, we will explore the concept of kids owning the learning, but it is important to note that when we say, "ownership of learning for all," we are talking about both kid learners and adult learners.

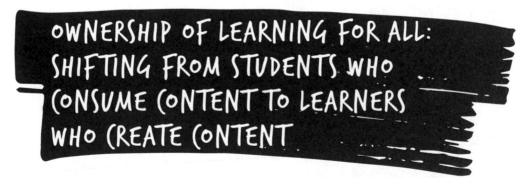

## OWNERSHIP OF LEARNING FOR ALL: SHIFTING FROM STUDENTS WHO CONSUME CONTENT TO LEARNERS WHO CREATE CONTENT

There is a famous scene in the movie *Ferris Bueller's Day Off* where an economics teacher, played by Ben Stein, delivers a very dull, monotone lecture and periodically says, "Anyone? Anyone?" in hopes that one of his students will chime in and provide an answer. Cut to students (intentional use of the word "students") staring blankly and one student actually sleeping (and drooling) at his desk. This scene resonates with those of us who have been tortured being passive participants in a lecture and completely disengaged as learners. Again, we admire and applaud the master teachers who can engage a group of kids in a traditional lecture, but this is not an example of one of those masters, nor do we think lecturing should comprise the majority of instructional time.

## Spectrum for Ownership of Learning

Let's think about "ownership of learning" on a spectrum. On one end of the spectrum, we have an extreme version of the teacher owning the learning. Absolutely all decisions about instruction and learning have been made by the teacher, the teacher is the focal point, and the students are passive participants. On the extreme opposite side, it is 100 percent learner driven. We are familiar with the teacher-driven side and granted, what was described is the extreme version, but what does the child learner having complete control of learning look like? Is there even a teacher present? Are there fellow learners involved? Sugata Mitra, educational researcher and winner of the 2013 TED Prize, has proven that kids can, in fact, teach themselves. In an experiment known as the "Hole in the Wall" project, Mitra (2012) and some of his colleagues placed a computer in the opening of a wall in Kalkaji, New Delhi. Via Edutopia, Mitra describes the experiment:

> The area was located in an expansive slum, with desperately poor people struggling to survive. The screen was visible from the street, and the PC was available to anyone who passed by. The computer had online access and a number of programs that could be used, but no instructions were given for its use.
>
> What happened next astonished us. Children came running out of the nearest slum and glued themselves to the computer. They couldn't get enough. They began to click and explore. They began to learn how to use this strange thing. A few hours later, a visibly surprised Vivek [friend of Mitra's] said the children were actually surfing the Web.

# OWNERSHIP OF LEARNING

**100% Teacher-Driven**

**100% Learner-Driven**

<<<<<<<<<<<<<<<<<<<<<  WHERE SHOULD WE BE?  >>>>>>>>>>>>>>>>>>>>>

*Source:* Photograph by Claudia Mufarrege: http://claudiomufarrege.daportfolio.com/; Since 2013, the NIIT Foundation, a not-for-profit organization, has been entrusted to implement the Hole-in-the-Wall Education Project (HiWEP) started by Dr. Sugata Mitra.

Mitra (2012) goes on to explain that after trying this experience in different parts of the world with different cultures, different languages, and different levels of education, the results were the same: "[T]he children were able to develop deep learning by teaching themselves." An advocate for child learner–driven inquiry, Mitra called this method of instruction *minimally invasive education (MIE),* and later work led to the term *self-organized learning environments (SOLEs).* Returning to the idea of "ownership of learning" on a spectrum, what does the middle look like to you? Is it constructivist? Do you call it project-based learning? Do you call it blended learning? All of the above? None of the above? While coming to consensus on where different instruction practices would land on the spectrum would be difficult, if not impossible, we find being conscious of the spectrum is critical.

As Sir Ken Robinson (2009) explains in his famous "Changing Education Paradigms" TED Talk, prior to the mid-19th century, there were no systems of public education, and there were many who believed that public education would fail because certain kids couldn't learn. Our hope is that there are no practicing educators who believe that. We believe that all kids can learn, and all kids can teach. However, our traditional, industrial model of education completely fails to leverage the unique strengths and talents of individuals and regardless of your lecturing skills, today's on-demand learners will be even less tolerant of learning that does not engage them than previous generations. The good news is that there are ways educators can make changes in their classroom starting now. As we will state numerous times throughout this book, there is never a "recipe" or one-size-fits-all solution for a classroom or school, but this section includes examples of strategies that have transformed learning in classrooms to empower ownership of learning for all.

## WE BELIEVE THAT ALL KIDS CAN LEARN, AND ALL KIDS CAN TEACH.

## Opportunities for Self-Directed Learning

In 2007, I (Lainie) made a visit to High Tech High (HTH) in San Diego that forever transformed my view of my role as a teacher. HTH opened in September 2000 as a public charter school and gained a lot of attention for success tied to the school's four connected design principles—equity, personalization, authentic work, and collaborative design. HTH was even featured in the thought-provoking documentary feature film, *Most Likely to Succeed*. In support of the school's design principle, equity, children are accepted by blind lottery by zip code, and they do not discriminate based on test scores or behavior. One of the many impressive statistics is that 100 percent of learners graduate HTH, and their college completion rate is almost 90 percent. What impressed me most, however, was the learning environment, which is personalized, project-based, and connected to the real world.

One of the classes I happened to walk into was building a boat. These learners are in a coastal city, San Diego, so a boat has relevance in their world, and think about the engineering, science, and math that goes into building one. This visit forever changed my mindset about my role as an educator because when we asked about their teacher selection process for a school with the word "tech" in the name, the director told us that the only technology question they ask prospective teachers is, "Are you willing to learn from your students?" At HTH, the learners are expected to find, evaluate, and recommend apps/devices and then teach the teacher and others how to use the tools. Prior to my visit to HTH, I was in the mindset that the teacher needed to be the expert on everything, which, of course, is an impossible task, especially given the abundance of information and tools as well as the diverse needs of learners.

As an educator who has taught adolescents as well as kindergarteners, first graders, and second graders, I wanted to explore what this would look like with younger, less independent learners. A kindergarten teacher let me borrow her class for a quick activity the first week of school. It was the first time these 5-year-olds had touched the tablets, and I did not provide any direct instruction on using them. Instead, I told them to take a device, and they had 4 minutes to figure out the features of the drawing app we would be using. At the end of 4 minutes, they needed to be prepared to teach me and the rest of the class something about the app. After everyone finished sharing, we all knew how to use the key features of the app. (Note: I use this strategy with adults too, but it often requires me encouraging risk-taking, something young children tend to do naturally.) Next, I gave the kindergartners a task. I asked them to show the number I said in manipulatives, use the device to take a photo of their work, check the quality of the photo, bring the photo into the drawing app, and then annotate their photo to demonstrate their knowledge. Their teacher thought I was insane. Following two-step directions is the expectation for kindergarten, and I just asked them to do much more than that. Plus, this school was in a very low socioeconomic area, and the teacher assumed that most, if not all, of her kids had never touched a device. My faith in the kids paid off as the vast majority of kids didn't have trouble completing all the steps, and those who did struggle looked over at a peer and quickly caught up.

Five-year-olds ask brilliant questions, they are great divergent thinkers, and what they lack in self-help skills they more than make up for as natural explorers, so we need to leverage that when we are designing learning experiences. Not only did these kids get a chance to teach others how to use the app and challenge themselves with five-step directions, but I, as the teacher, also learned a lot about the kids really quickly. Most children did what I expected, but some kids didn't just write the number; they wrote an equation like 2+5=7. One child, Micah, actually wrote the equation both ways, 2+5=7 and 5+2=7. Others struggled just to count out 7. I had them save their work and share it with their teacher so she could review later. This was just the first step in a cycle of inquiry for that teacher and her group of learners. We were accessing the current state. Next, their teacher would go on to analyze their work to see where each learner was in relation to the learning objectives, and she would gather strategies for helping those who were struggling. Here is the beautiful part of learning from kids: Before she even opens a book or clicks on a website to get those strategies, she leverages the resources in the room, her learners. This goes back to the section on Peer Instruction. Is there a 5-year-old in the room who understands it and can explain it in a way that makes sense to another 5-year-old? In the cycle of inquiry, that teacher needs to plan ways to leverage the learners in the room, implement, and gather data, and the cycle starts again. By providing the conditions for learning and having faith in our kids, we give ourselves space to truly watch, listen, and—most importantly— learn from our kids. We learn how to improve our practice and how to meet their needs.

Many learners like the opportunity to figure it out, and they like the opportunity to teach others. I debrief with learners after I do an activity like this, and here are some typical things they enjoy about it:

- The challenge
- Creating/being creative
- Learning something new
- Collaborating
- Overcoming fear

It is our experience that kids are curious, they want to learn, and they also want to teach. We should empower them to do so!

## Instructional Practices That Empower Learners of All Ages

*Source:* unsplash.com/@heidisandstrom

The three of us have spent the latter parts of our careers focused on innovative learning experiences. That is to say, we seek out innovative and sustainable ways to transform teaching and learning to empower our kids and amplify learning. Sometimes we get labeled as "ed techies," but that is not our focus. We do not allow ourselves to get distracted by shiny new devices and apps with endless bells and whistles. We want learning experiences for kids to be personalized, inspiring, engaging, and empowering. Kids are always our focus, and creating the best possible learning experiences for them, that is our true north. It just so happens that emerging instructional practices that leverage technology to empower learners are often our best option.

What follows are just a few of those learner-driven practices, but please note that this list is in no way exhaustive, and there is often overlap between the different models. For example, empowering the learner by giving them voice and choice is a common thread that runs throughout all of these practices. Also, many innovative schools use more than one of these practices as part of a comprehensive instructional program. For example, a STEM/STEAM school might be using project-based learning and a form of blended learning to personalize learning and free up face-to-face time for inquiry-based learning experiences. At the heart of all of these instructional practices are learning experiences that empower learners and give adults an opportunity to learn with and from kids.

### Project-Based Learning (PBL)

According to the Buck Institute for Education (BIE.org), a foremost authority on PBL, "Project Based Learning is a teaching method in which students gain knowledge and skills by working for an extended period of time to investigate and respond to an authentic, engaging, and complex question, problem, or challenge." This model aligns with the *high-quality PBL (HQPBL)* framework, which includes six criteria:

- Intellectual challenge and accomplishment
- Authenticity
- Public product
- Collaboration
- Project management
- Reflection

These learning experiences are inquiry-based and the process is dynamic, allowing for iteration in solving real-world problems while developing deeper knowledge. It is important to note that the teacher's role is critical—not as a "sage on the stage," but rather more of a "meddler in the middle." In PBL, teachers strategically and minimalistically insert themselves, not to rescue the learner, but to encourage and guide along the way.

### Competency-Based Learning (CBL)

iNACOL (inacol.org), a leading advocate for transforming learning, in partnership with their CompetencyWorks project and the innovators involved, have developed a working definition of *competency-based learning*:

- Students advance upon demonstrated mastery.
- Competencies include explicit, measurable, transferable learning objectives that empower students.
- Assessment is meaningful and a positive learning experience for students.
- Students receive timely, differentiated support based on their individual learning needs.
- Learning outcomes emphasize competencies that include application and creation of knowledge, along with the development of important skills and dispositions.

More simply put, CBL, also known as mastery-based, performance-based, and proficiency-based learning, is about mastery of learning targets, not seat time, and to do that, we need to redesign the education system to focus on actual student learning in order to prepare our kids for their future.

## Blended Learning

*Blended learning* is an instructional model in which the learner participates in instruction both online and in a supervised brick-and-mortar location away from home. The learning experience can happen entirely in a traditional setting, or it may be a combination of both at school and at home. The key is that the learner has at least some element of control over the time, place, path, or pace, and the learning experiences are integrated. The learning is highly personalized with the teacher carefully designing which experiences take place online and which experiences take place face-to-face. The Blended Learning Universe (blendedlearning.org), curated by the Clayton Christensen Institute, is packed with resources, including practical guides, video tutorials, work-sheets, and a directory of blended learning programs worldwide. Important to note: Blended learning is also a great approach to personalize professional learning!

## Universal Design for Learning (UDL)

CAST is the nonprofit education research and development organization behind the *universal design for learning (UDL)*. CAST defines UDL as "a research-based framework to improve and optimize teaching and learning for all people based on scientific insights into how humans learn." The three principles of UDL are engagement, representation, and action and expression.

The history of UDL goes back as far as 1984 and over the years, guidelines were developed as a tool to support educators in putting the framework into practice. According to their website (cast.org), "The goal of UDL is to support learners to become 'expert learners' who are, each in their own way, purposeful and motivated, resourceful and knowledgeable, and strategic and goal driven." Making a connection to social-emotional learning (SEL), a theme that runs throughout this book, the "engagement" principle in UDL focuses on *affective networks,* the "why" of learning.

Again, these are just a few of the learner-driven practices that have been identified, and the fact that there is no "recipe" cannot be overstated. Equifinality is a reality in education. There is no one way to get good results. However, to actually get good results requires effective professional learning in a cycle of inquiry. Unfortunately, what often happens when districts or schools decide to adopt one or more of these practices is that teachers are all pulled together for a "sit and get." As we will discuss in greater detail in Chapter 2, "Peers," workshops are not inherently evil. Workshops are in fact an opportunity to bring a community of educators together to discuss and explore new ideas with the support of leadership, coaches, and team members—our peers. Workshops can be a starting point, but one-time workshops alone are completely insufficient, especially for major shifts like to the learner-driven practices shared above. Administrators and teachers need to cocreate ongoing, job-embedded opportunities to be constant, reflective learners.

A cycle of inquiry provides the structure, and the learning relationships provide "critical friends" to reflect with and, with fidelity, iterate based on the impact that the data show. For example, project-based learning (PBL) is a powerful methodology, yet we also know that implementation of PBL is very inconsistent. This often has to do with ongoing support or lack thereof. After the PBL workshop, what comes next? Does a teacher who usually lectures and asks all the questions magically shift from "sage on the stage" to "meddler in the middle" without a plan and support? Not likely. Further, how does he or she measure the impact of a new practice? We need cycles of inquiry—yes, "cycles," plural. While the kids are engaged in a learner-driven cycle of inquiry about the content, the teacher is engaged in a cycle of inquiry about the efficacy of the practice.

Through a cycle of inquiry, the teacher or team of teachers first identifies the *focus,* and that focus needs to be the right grain size. As we noted above, in PBL, teachers "strategically and minimalistically insert themselves." Thus, after analyzing current practices, a focus that would be a good grain size would be something like "classroom culture," "guiding inquiry," or "managing teamwork." Also, rather than starting with a 3-month long PBL unit, the teachers might begin with a shorter unit that gives them a chance to iterate before implementing an extended PBL unit.

Leveraging the PBL samples and resources from the workshop, teachers then identify what else they need to "learn" in order to plan for implementing this practice in a way that is appropriate for their learners. In an evolving learner cycle of inquiry, the "focus" is personalized and the "learn" element is also personalized, as a kindergarten teacher and a high school teacher have very different learners, and an introductory PBL workshop may not have provided specifics for an early elementary classroom. A kindergarten teacher who is focused on "guiding inquiry" in PBL might decide to use a question-generating protocol such as the Question Formulation Technique (QFT) previously discussed, but the protocol needs to be adapted for younger learners, so the teacher needs to reach out to our *peers* and *the world* to learn strategies for the primary classroom.

Once the teacher has developed a plan, it is implemented, and this is the opportunity to "refine," both on the fly and after reviewing data. This is known as formative assessment. For example, initially the teacher asks the learners to get into small groups to verbally generate questions, but the teacher quickly realizes that the directions were not explained well, and the kids don't understand to "ask as many questions as you can." The teacher pulls the group back together and asks the kids to think of one question and, instead of getting into small groups, turn to the person next to them and share their question. The teacher then directs the learners, "Once each of you shares your first question, keep going with as many questions as you can until we get back together." The teacher circulates around the room, listening to individuals' questions and learning from the questions the kids ask. When the teacher gets the group back together, partners share out their questions to the whole group while the teacher transcribes them. Just like Melissa did in the vignette shared earlier, the teacher uses the questions to refine practice and plan next steps. The entire process is reflective, but we also need to reach out to our "critical friends," our *peers* and *the world,* to validate the efficacy of our practice before shifting our focus to a different practice such as "self-assessment" in PBL. This is just one simple example of learning from and with kids in a cycle of inquiry with the overarching idea that when we set goals and continually measure the impact of our actions, we will continually come closer to achieving our personal best. We will go more into depth on this in the chapters that follow.

There are so many innovative educators rethinking what learning looks like. One of our favorite examples of learning from kids is Eric Marcos and the website, mathtrain.tv, that his community of learners created. It all started back in 2006, when Eric got a new PC tablet in his classroom, and he did something he would never regret: He trusted his kids and asked them to help him figure out how this new, fancy device worked. (Note, this is a year before the iPhone was even announced and years before iPads hit the market.)

Many of you will have heard of Khan Academy and the video tutorials that Khan created to teach. Right around the time Khan Academy launched, Eric Marcos and his learners were creating their own video tutorial library. When Eric decided to use his new tech skills (acquired in large part through his kids teaching him) to create a quick video tutorial to help a learner with his homework, he soon realized that his learners really wanted video tutorials to learn from and, more than that, they wanted to make their own to teach others! So Eric took his trust in his learners even further and, in addition to letting his kids help him figure out the device, he actually let them use it on their own to create tutorials. Eric recalls, "I loved making tutorials. But after our first student one in 2007, I was basically put out of a job" (personal communication). The following vignette describes the impact on Eric's practice as well as the learning community in general as he evolved to learn from kids.

# LEARNING FROM KIDS IN ACTION: EMPOWERING LEARNERS

Eric Marcos
*Mathematics Teacher*
*Lincoln Middle School*
*Santa Monica, CA*

*Could you describe how watching the content that your kids create helps you in your cycle of inquiry to improve instruction?*

A simple example was watching students explain how to divide fractions. They would show how you just "flip and multiply by the reciprocal." They would get the correct answer, but when asked, the students would not be able to explain why we flip and multiply by the reciprocal. Once I realized that students could get A's on fraction tests, yet have no clue why or what was happening when they would flip and multiply by the reciprocal, I knew I needed to find a different way to teach that concept. I researched and tested different strategies and completely transformed that lesson. I now have an informative, visual lesson on dividing fractions, and the video tutorials that the learners create demonstrate their true understanding of the mathematics reasoning, not just a regurgitation of steps. This is now one of my favorite lessons.

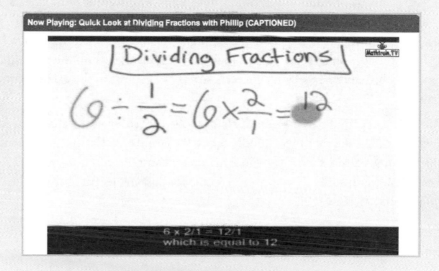

*(Continued)*

*What other benefits have you seen from your learners creating content to teach others?*

"Kid Language"—One of my students, "Paul," mentioned how the student tutorials are great because they are in the "kid language." It's not yet another adult explaining the same thing, the same way. Plus, when I, as an educator, hear the "kid language," I'm learning new ways to explain the concepts.

Another benefit I have seen is when students stop mid-video because they realized they don't understand why they are doing a particular step. Sometimes the students abandon the video, go research or find out whatever they were unsure of, and come back later to redo the video. Other times they might ask me or another student for clarification before they continue recording. They are so motivated to do their best. It is an amazing experience watching a student self-edit or do a second take because he or she was not satisfied with the way something was written or explained. I don't think you often see students doing that with traditional homework and all of this informs my instruction and helps me grow as a learner.

*How has this impacted the families of your kids?*

Oops—Initially, it disrupted the after-school schedules of some families. Students would get so engrossed in their work and forget to tell their folks they were staying after school. At least once a week, around 4 or 5 P.M., frantic parents or guardians would come running into our classroom exclaiming that they had been looking for their kid! I think I got a bunch of students in trouble throughout the years. Now, I make absolutely sure the students contact their parent or guardian when staying after. It's so easy to get lost in the excitement of creating tutorials!

Pride—We have had proud parents/guardians sit in the classroom and watch their kid finish up a tutorial. Families like that their middle school kid wants to stay in a mathematics class after school! Bonus: Family members who don't understand the content and can't help their child at home use Mathtrain.TV as a resource. It is not just me learning from kids; families are learning from their kids too!

It is important to highlight that, in addition to the video tutorials helping the kids learn and Eric grow in his practice, these video tutorials also help families understand *how* their child is learning a concept in school. In recent years, there has been a growing debate on the value of homework, and it may not get settled anytime soon, but consider this:

- Do your learners have access to someone at home who can help when they are struggling with content?
- Do your learners' families know how to explain concepts using the current strategies?
- If your learners' families don't know current strategies, are your learners actually prepared to explain?

These are points of friction for homework that have been eliminated in Eric's community of learners because he has empowered his kids to teach. Even if his kids don't have someone at home who can explain the concept using the current strategies, even if a particular child can't explain it her- or himself, they have a whole library filled with video tutorials from other kids using "kid language" who can teach it.

Clearly, the content that Eric's learners have created has made an impact well beyond the four walls of his classroom. In fact, Mathtrain.TV has been featured and aired in 155 countries, in 11 languages. He has empowered his learners to be master teachers. They are expert explainers, educating their teachers and their families as well as kids and adults around the world.

## Ownership of Learning for All: Social and Emotional Learning (SEL)

As discussed in the Introduction, the three of us, along with many other educators, believe that social-emotional learning (SEL) is an essential piece that is ongoing in the learning culture. It is a strand throughout this book and in this next section, we intentionally highlight an example of how we can learn from kids regarding classroom/school climate and its impacts on learning.

> "Adults don't give students voice or agency; it's not ours to give. Students already have these, and it's up to us to listen and provide access and opportunities to use it."
> —Jessica Hoffman, Yale Center for Emotional Intelligence

There should be no question that #EmotionsMatter. Any teacher who has spent time with even one child who has suffered trauma knows that. Even if you haven't worked with a child who has suffered severe trauma, you have more than likely worked with a child who struggled with a less-than-ideal home life, bullying at school, or some other challenges that caused stress and anxiety. We, as educators, need to do all that we can to develop socially and emotionally healthy kids. Beyond the humanitarian reasons for SEL, we also need to focus on SEL because, as a wealth of research shows, it directly impacts the efficacy of teaching and learning. Sadly, in education, the stress of high-stakes testing and achievement has us ignoring the research, focusing solely on the cognitive domain and neglecting the affective domain.

Fortunately, in recent years, SEL has been getting some much-deserved attention, which has led to increased availability of educational resources. One of the best examples we have seen comes from a collaborative effort between the Yale Center for Emotional Intelligence, Facebook, and Lady Gaga's Born This Way Foundation, which led to the creation of InspirED (inspired.fb.com). InspirED provides free resources, designed by teens, educators, and SEL experts, to empower kids to work together to create a more positive school climate and foster greater well-being in their schools and communities. InspirED is an example of the importance of both emotional intelligence in education and learning from and with kids.

According to Julie McGarry, program manager for inspirED at Yale Center for Emotional Intelligence, the massive Emotion Revolution study, referenced earlier in this section, revealed that while the majority of students said they felt *tired*, *stressed*, and *bored*, they also discovered that what kids *hoped* to feel was largely about being actively engaged.

When the three of us see the kids' words in the image on the right, we think "ownership of learning for all." SEL is an amazing opportunity for learning to be truly reciprocal between the adults and kids! Next, we will share Grossmont High School's story, focusing on how they are learning from kids by leveraging learning relationships in an ongoing cycle of inquiry that empowers kids and adults to own social and emotional learning. In these vignettes, a high school student as well as an adult learner share their experiences with inspirED.

# WHAT DO KIDS HOPE TO FEEL AT SCHOOL?

Energized and motivated
Empowered and inspired
Happy and excited
Passionate and purposeful
Respected and valued

# LEARNING FROM KIDS IN ACTION: INSPIRED

**Kennedy Dirkes**
*Senior*
*Grossmont High School*
*San Diego County, CA*

*How have your experiences with inspirED led to learning that is reciprocal between adults and kids?*

Working with InspirED has differed from my other learning experiences because my voice gets heard. It is a platform that helps me follow through with my ideas and produce them myself or with a team of other students. Through InspirED, I have been able to create a common language on campus, which has slowly trickled into teacher classrooms. This common language has helped lower the communication barrier between teachers and students, thus creating a more inviting atmosphere for the student's voice.

By implementing InspirED on our campus, we have slowly seen a change in the relationship between teachers and students. For example, I have had test dates and due dates moved due to teachers listening to students' needs and compromising.

When learning is reciprocal between students and teachers, it creates relationships. These relationships lead to a more enjoyable classroom experience on both the learning and teaching side of education.

*Your school is very active on social media. What does it mean to you to have an audience outside your school, where you can share your voice and teach others around the world?*

Having an audience outside of school has been an unreal experience. Being able to share my projects to inspire other teachers and students continues to motivate me to cultivate change on my campus. If I can do it, why can't they?

*What would you say to educators to encourage them to learn from and with kids?*

Allow students to be the main focus and heads of a project. Ideas that come from students, raw and without adult influence, will help you understand what students want to change within their community.

Jeremy Hersch
*Social Science Teacher and ASB Advisor*
*Grossmont High School*

*How have your experiences with inspirED led to learning that is reciprocal between adults and kids?*

I am not a 16-year-old anymore. There is no way I will ever know what it feels like to be a student in my class. Listening to student voices and empowering students to share their story is the only way I could find to truly understand what my students were feeling. It was a humbling and eye-opening experience.

Last year, when brainstorming ideas for our campus, the students involved in InspirED decided they wanted to make a lesson for our staff to teach. They came up with a lesson about what it feels like to participate in class from the student perspective. They wanted our staff to understand the pressure students feel to participate and how it feels when they do not know the answer, the perceived ridicule from their classmates and embarrassment from not knowing the answer to a question.

Teachers must be able to listen and hear the voice of their students to understand how they are feeling. It is the first step to building a relationship. Without a relationship, it is nearly impossible to be an effective teacher.

*What, if any, concerns did you have about giving up control and allowing kids to teach? And how did those concerns resolve (if they did)?*

Again, relationships are key. Shifting power to students can be a challenge when you need to take control of the classroom back. Having clear norms and rock-solid relationships is a critical element to have in place before turning teaching over to students. We now have many teachers who have adopted the InspirED SEL–based model in their rooms. They have seen fantastic results learning from and with their students!

## LOOKING AHEAD

We believe that kids are not only the purpose for absolutely everything we do in education, but they are also the best resource we have. By honoring kids and giving them opportunities to lead the learning and including them in our professional learning, we not only leverage them as a resource, but we also prepare them for the real world by cultivating the leadership and learning skills that will be required throughout their life. So ask yourself, what can you learn from kids? Use the space at the end of the chapter to reflect on examples shared in this section. Make a list, draw your own cycle of inquiry, and so on.

## LEARNING FROM KIDS KEY IDEAS

| | |
|---|---|
| **Unlearn, Then Relearn Your Role** | Most of us grew up with someone at the front of the room working very hard, but the time has come to shift from genius to *scenius,* leveraging the unique gifts (knowledge, skills, and dispositions) of all learners. |
| **What Are They Thinking?** | Leverage strategies and tools to make thinking transparent as you and your learners engage in a cycle of inquiry that guides instruction and informs your practice. |
| **Ownership of Learning for All** | Think about "ownership of learning" on a spectrum. Where are you and your learners on this spectrum? In what ways can you shift from students who consume content to learners who create content? |
| **Learning From Kids Starts With Listening to Kids** | As Adora says, "Have informal conversations with kids in small groups about important issues. It might surprise you how full of opinions kids can be. Try asking kids about friendship, beauty, happiness, love." |
| **See It From a Kid's Perspective** | See your learning environments and experiences as a kid sees them. This keeps you learner-focused. One strategy that some principals have adopted is periodically shadowing a kid for a day (#ShadowAStudent). Be the learner that gets on the bus early in the morning, arrives at school, goes to class(es), goes to lunch, goes back to class(es), goes home on the bus, and does the homework. If you've ever been in a 6-hour workshop and walked away exhausted from intense learning with minimal breaks, consider this: That is a typical school day for most kids. Starting with kids is the best way to find a focus for your cycle of inquiry. |

| LEARNING FROM KIDS KEY IDEAS | |
|---|---|
| **Develop a Plan for Embedding Inquiry Into Your Practice** | Develop a detailed, concrete plan to implement a new practice that makes thinking transparent to tailor instruction and promotes inquiry in your practice. In Carol Dweck's bestseller, *Mindset: The New Psychology of Success,* she shares research by Peter Gollwitzer and his colleagues that shows that vowing, even intense vowing, is often useless. |
| | Think about it in vivid details: |
| | When will you follow through on your plan? |
| | Where will it take place? |
| | How will you execute your plan? |
| **Find Your Focus** | We often get many great ideas at once. Our kids, peers, and the world inspire us, but pick one area of focus for your cycle of inquiry and make a list of additional focus areas to cover down the road! Then, set yourself a future reminder for 30 days from now, 2 months from now, etc. When you get the reminder, reevaluate your list and prioritize based on the current needs. |

# LEARN MORE FROM THOUGHT LEADERS WHO INSPIRE US TO LEARN FROM KIDS

## Read:

Bryk, A. S., Gomez, L. M., Grunow, A., & LeMahieu, P. G. (2016). *Learning to improve: How America's schools can get better at getting better.* Cambridge, MA: Harvard Education Press.

Hattie, J. (2009). *Visible learning.* Thousand Oaks, CA: Corwin.

Learning Forward Standards for Professional Learning: *Resources, Learning Designs, Outcomes, and Data* (learningforward.org)

Marzano, R. J. (2017). *The new art and science of teaching (more than fifty new instructional strategies for academic success).* Bloomington, IN: Solution Tree.

Resnick, M. (2017). *Lifelong kindergarten.* Cambridge: The MIT Press.

Rothstein, D., & Santana, L. (2014). *Make just one change: Teach students to ask their own questions.* Cambridge, MA: Harvard Education Press.

Sheninger, E. C., & Murray, T. C. (2017). *Learning transformed: 8 keys to designing tomorrow's schools, today.* Alexandria, VA: ASCD.

## Watch:

Adora Svitak: What Adults Can Learn From Kids (2010). TED Talk (ted.com/talks/adora_svitak)

Sugata Mitra: Build a School in the Cloud. (2013). TED Talk (ted.com/talks/sugata_mitra_build_a_school_in_the_cloud)

Alan November: What Is the Value of a Teacher? (2016). TEDxWestVancouverED (youtu.be/BN4c0EqY61o)

## Listen:

The Cult of Pedagogy podcast (cultofpedagogy.com/pod)

## Explore:

Visit evolvinglearning.org for more.

# THOUGHTS, JOTS, AND NEXT STEPS

# CHAPTER 2

## LEARNING FROM PEERS

is about
### honoring the learner

and cultivating an inquiry-driven culture of ownership and empowerment

## PEERS

are engaged in

### WORKSHOPS
that define the schoolwide focus & initiate a collective cycle of inquiry

### PLCs
that provide job-embedded recurring cycles of collective inquiry

### COACHING
that provides mentors to support individuals in their cycles of inquiry

### SOCIAL-EMOTIONAL LEARNING
is the foundation and lens through which both kid and adult learning is designed.

# HONOR THE LEARNER: PEERS

In the previous chapter, "Learning From Kids," we discussed the concept of who works harder in a classroom, the teacher or the student. The vast majority of people would agree that in a traditional classroom, the teacher works harder. Think of how this parallels teacher learners in traditional PD (i.e., workshops, trainings, inservices).

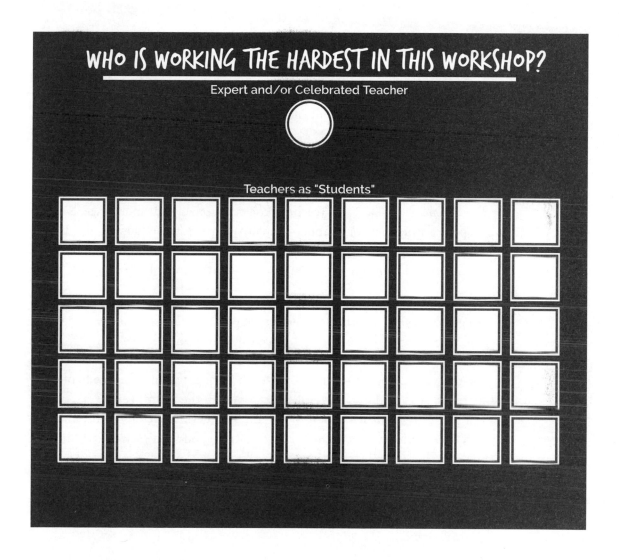

Just as we critically examined the traditional teaching model used in our classrooms, we also need to look at how we, as educators, are learning. Teacher learners in traditional workshops take on the role of student, and their role is frequently, if not entirely, passive compared to their role in their own classrooms. In traditional workshops or keynotes, an expert or celebrated teacher is usually in front of the room while a group of teachers is doing "sit and get." Typically, in such settings, the learners have little in the way of choice. To be clear, we know the intentions are good (after all, no one wants to intentionally provide "bad" PD), but this seems antithetical to many of the shifts we are attempting to make in our classrooms.

A major part of the problem is that resource limitations such as time and money become barriers to effective adult learning that aren't fair to kids or the dedicated teachers who serve them. While we know that time can be a challenge in providing high-quality professional learning, we question if money is really a barrier. In 2014, when the Bill and Melinda Gates Foundation contracted with the Boston Consulting Group to research professional development for teachers, the report, *Teachers Know Best,* found that $18 billion was spent annually on teacher PD across the nation (k12education.gatesfoundation.org). In 2015, *The Mirage: Confronting the Hard Truth About Our Quest for Teacher Development* by The New Teacher Project revealed that on average, $18,000 is spent per teacher for training annually (tntp.org/assets/documents/TNTP-Mirage_2015.pdf). Therefore, the problem may be less about limited financial resources and more about how this money has traditionally been spent.

In traditional PD, the solution for limited time and money is typically a "one-size-fits-all" approach where a group of teachers spanning a wide variety of learners and content are placed into the same space to learn at the exact same pace following the exact same path. Sadly, this does not account for the very complex room full of teachers and the unique needs of their learners. Also, it doesn't leverage the *scenius* in the room. Teachers truly are unique individuals with their own unique gifts (knowledge, skills, and dispositions), and we have so much to learn from and with each other! Much in the way that we are struggling to abandon a "factory" approach to teaching and learning in which all kids are expected to learn the same thing at the same pace, we are striving to personalize professional learning, and some of the best opportunities can be found in the collaborative models described in this chapter.

# CURRENT SPENDING ON "PD"

## $18 BILLION

spent annually on teachers'
PD across the nation

## $18,000

spent annually per teacher
for training

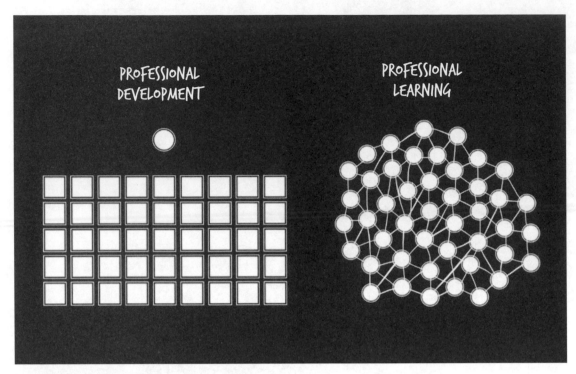

PROFESSIONAL DEVELOPMENT

PROFESSIONAL LEARNING

Inspired by Austin Kleon

active applicable authentic badges blended brave buy-in
choice
collaborative creative customized data
differentiated digestible distributive diverse dynamic
empower energizing exciting enlightening
engaging
flexible fun goal-based hands-on
helpful implemented important individualized informative
innovative inspiring interactive
interest-based interesting interactive learner-focused
meaningful memorable modern needed not eye-gougingly
loving ongoing participatory passion personal
poses practical product professional purposeful realistic relax
relevant research-based respectful self-directed self-
selected social man standards-driven
student-centered support sustainable
teacher-led tools useful valued varied vision voice

We recently asked a large group of educators, "What words describe what professional learning should look like?" and turned their responses into a word cloud. The size of each word depends on the frequency it was shared. The larger the word, the more often it was used.

If you are reading this book on personalizing professional learning, words like "choice," "engaging," and "relevant" probably resonate with you. If you are a classroom teacher, you may feel like you have not been given a lot of "choice" on your learning experiences. If you are a principal, district administrator, or superintendent, you may feel like you want choice, engagement, and relevance for yourself and your team, but where do you start?

## Adult Learning Theory

Before we share possible solutions for the lack of resources and other challenges that most of us face, let's revisit Malcolm Knowles's best practices for adult learning. Knowles, a pioneer and expert on *andragogy,* the art and science of adult learning, provided his Four Principles of Andragogy in 1984b:

1. Adults need to be involved in the planning and evaluation of their instruction (Choice).

2. Experience (including mistakes) provides the basis for the learning activities (Hands-on).

3. Adults are most interested in learning subjects that have immediate relevance and impact to their job or personal life (Personalized).

4. Adult learning is problem-centered rather than content-oriented (Inquiry-driven). (Kearsley, 2010)

Consider the correlation between Knowles's four principles and the word cloud responses. How many parallels can you find?

## Cycle of Inquiry for Professional Learning

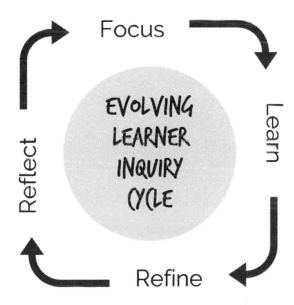

As discussed in Chapter 1, to be effective, an educator's cycle of inquiry must be continuous and must include kids, peers, and the world. We also discussed how kids are engaged in a cycle of inquiry for deeper learning of the content, while adults are engaged in a cycle of inquiry to improve their practice. We believe that both are critical, and we hope they are practiced in harmony. We designed the Evolving Learner Cycle of Inquiry to work for both kids and adults, but it is also helpful to examine specific models that provide additional information for specific situations. In Chapter 1, "Learning From Kids," we explored the 5 E's instructional model (Engage, Explore, Explain, Elaborate, and Evaluate). As we explore cycles of inquiry for professional learning, we will focus on two, Jim Knight's Impact Cycle (in the section on instructional coaching) and Learning Forward's Cycle of Continuous Improvement.

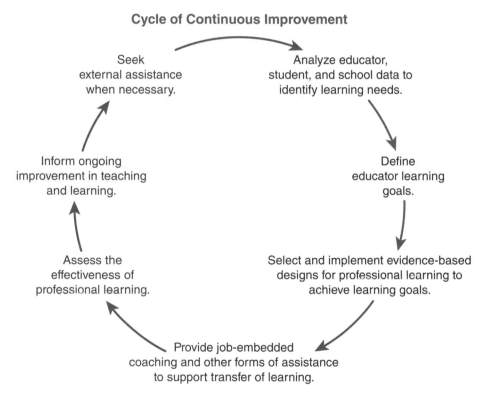

**Cycle of Continuous Improvement**

Seek external assistance when necessary.

Analyze educator, student, and school data to identify learning needs.

Inform ongoing improvement in teaching and learning.

Define educator learning goals.

Assess the effectiveness of professional learning.

Select and implement evidence-based designs for professional learning to achieve learning goals.

Provide job-embedded coaching and other forms of assistance to support transfer of learning.

*Source:* Learning Forward, "A Cycle of Continuous Improvement." Retrieved September 2019 from https://learningforward.org/docs/default-source/publicationssection/Transform/tool-cycle-of-continuous-improvement.pdf?sfvrsn=0

## Cycle of Continuous Improvement

Learning Forward's "Implementation Standard for Professional Learning" states that we need to "integrate constructive feedback and reflection to support continuous improvement in practice that allows educators to move along a continuum from novice to expert through application of their professional learning" (learningforward.org/standards/implementation/).

The Cycle of Continuous Improvement is also aligned with the Evolving Learner Cycle of Inquiry: focus, learn, refine, reflect. In addition, it includes details specific to learning from peers such as, "Provide job-embedded coaching."

As we analyze the two cycles, the parallels are clear. In the context of evolving learning, we want to reiterate that these cycles of inquiry for professional learning are most effective when they include kids, peers, and the world. For example, in Chapter 1, "Learning From Kids," we explored practices for empowering ownership of learning for all, and we shared how Eric Marcos empowered his learners to create their own video tutorial library. Those video tutorials are a powerful resource for learners, but equally important, they help Eric identify learner-focused goals in his cycle of inquiry to improve instruction.

Furthermore, achieving our learner-focused goals may require us to seek external assistance. We extend our knowledge base exponentially when we go beyond our classroom, our school site, and even our district. In Chapter 3, "Learning From the World," we will explore the unlimited possibilities for on-demand learning. When we leverage the knowledge, skills, and dispositions of *kids, peers,* and *the world,* we all benefit.

## Cultivating a Culture of Ownership and Empowerment

If money isn't the primary issue and we understand adult learning theory, where do we start? Education leaders, including but not limited to classroom teachers, instruction coaches/mentors, principals, and districtwide administrators, need to strive to achieve Learning Forward's Leadership Standard for Professional Learning, which calls on "skillful leaders who develop capacity, advocate, and create support systems for professional learning." For some schools, this requires a significant culture shift. In the book *Learning Transformed: 8 Keys to Designing Tomorrow's Schools, Today,* Eric C. Sheninger and Tom C. Murray (2017) provide 10 specific ways to foster a learning culture of ownership and empowerment:

1. Clearly define and articulate the vision.
2. Model: Practice what you preach.

3. Learning should be anytime, anywhere.

4. Balance districtwide initiatives with the need for learning that's personal.

5. Move from hours-based to outcome-based accountability.

6. Shift the culture of professional learning.

7. Empower staff to design their own learning.

8. Solicit teacher feedback.

9. Break down silos: Cross-district collaboration.

10. Grow your network.

The work of Learning Forward as well as Sheninger and Murray provides the mindset necessary for a learning community to move forward in inquiry-driven professional learning from kids, peers, and the world.

Just like the previous chapter, this one will focus on learning relationships and research-based strategies to improve our practice through an ongoing cycle of inquiry. The overarching idea is that by setting goals and continually measuring the impact of your actions, you will continually come closer to achieving your personal best. While there are many models and a wide range of terminology to describe such cycles, there are several core principles that run through virtually every variation.

1. Determining a learner-**FOCUS**ed goal (often with a coach) or "problem of practice" (POP).

   An example of a goal is, *Ninety percent of my learners will be able to identify and describe the main ideas of a text.* An example of a problem of practice is, *Many of our learners tune out when we study primary historical documents. What can we do to enhance levels of engagement?* Typically, teams develop theories of action to help solve these POPs.

2. Collecting and analyzing data to measure the impact of changes that teachers have enacted (**LEARN**)

3. **REFINE**-ing practices with the intent of coming increasingly closer to meeting the stated objective(s)

4. Sharing results and determining next steps (**REFLECT**)

This chapter will offer variations on this framework as well as strategies and examples, but just as there is no recipe for learning from kids, there is no recipe for learning from peers. First and foremost, this is about a mindset—the mindset that you can always improve your practice, and your peers can help you do that.

> "The work we do with our students and our colleagues in our classrooms, in our own schools—that work is our art. No one can give us the recipe for how to make that art. Rather, we create it day in and day out, in response to the particular content and in collaboration with the particular individuals with whom we work."
>
> —Tina Blythe

We must admit that this chapter on *learning from peers* was by far the most difficult to write! The current roles of all three of us have been focused on being instructional leaders and coaches. We are so immersed in this concept that we didn't know where to start and what grain size was right for each topic. We reread both seminal and current research. We devoured the latest books on PLCs, coaching, and anything we could find that focused on learning from peers, all the while keenly aware of the challenge of devoting a single chapter to all of these topics. We also are mindful that these topics—and the concept of learning from peers in general—have emotional resonance that is rooted in the fear of admitting that we are not perfect. Whatever your role in education, it is not an easy thing to lay your cards on the table and be vulnerable to your peers. We truly get that. However, the amazing thing about most educators is that we care about our kids enough to put our egos aside and do what is in their best interests. For the minority of educators not willing to do so, that does not make them bad people, but we do hope they find happiness in another profession because our kids need teachers who never stop learning, never stop improving.

> "If we create a culture where every teacher believes they need to improve, not because they are not good enough but because they can be even better, there is no limit to what we can achieve."
>
> —Dylan Wiliam

Yes, this chapter was a challenge, but, as we shared at the beginning, we didn't choose to write this book because we had all the answers, but rather, because we wanted to find the answers.

## Shifting From Professional Development to Professional Learning

Now that we've addressed some key ingredients in learning from peers, let's talk about *how.* How do we shift from PD to personalized professional learning (PL) and not have it break the bank or consume our every waking moment? As we move through this section, we will share a variety of solutions. Some solutions can be quickly and easily implemented, working within current structures, and other solutions are more disruptive and require careful implementation. All of these solutions are focused on learners' needs (both kids' and adults') through cycles of inquiry. It is critical to have a mindset focused on learners as we renovate and, in some cases, demolish and completely rebuild adult learning experiences.

## WORKSHOPS THAT WORK: RENOVATING THE ONE-SIZE-FITS-ALL MODEL

Arguably the most common form of PD is the after-school or all-day workshop. While it may surprise you, we are not advocating for the total abolishment of these. In *Unmistakable Impact: A Partnership Approach for Dramatically Improving Instruction,* Jim Knight (2011) explains, "workshops can be highly effective for introducing ideas into a system so long as those ideas are translated into practice through the assistance of instructional coaches and other forms of follow-up" (p. 133). In Chapter 1, we discussed how workshops were an opportunity to bring a community of educators together to discuss and explore new ideas. Some innovative schools even involve kids in workshops to encourage ownership of learning and job-embedded support. Unfortunately, strategies like that are not the norm, and what is often overlooked in planning a workshop is a plan for the application of new knowledge/content/skills. How will we put these newly acquired concepts, skills, and dispositions into practice? What will we be doing between now and the next time we get together as a team (schoolwide or department/grade level) to work on this topic? What are the deliverables to move toward collective efficacy? To be perfectly clear, it doesn't matter how good the workshop is—without follow-up, there is at best a five to ten percent chance the professional learning will lead to change in our practice (Joyce & Showers, 2002). We must balance the work that brings a school/district community of educators together to introduce new ideas (workshops) and teamwork (PLCs and coaching) that takes those concepts and applies them in classrooms.

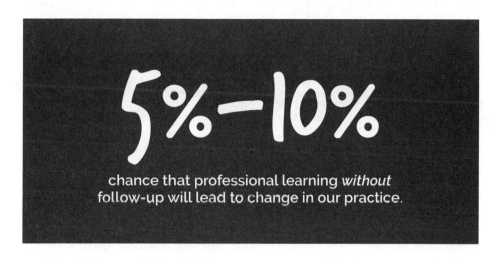

**5%–10%**

chance that professional learning *without* follow-up will lead to change in our practice.

In addition to planning for ongoing support, we also advocate for rethinking and renovating the format. What prework can be done to level the group up and truly utilize the face-to-face learning? Where does online learning fit in? Can it be used to offer flexibility/choice, allowing individuals and teams to choose pathways that are best for them? Before you plan the next workshop, review the Learning Forward standards as well as Sheninger and Murray's "Ownership and Empowerment" practices, referenced previously in this chapter, and adjust as necessary. There can be great value in bringing different groups together to learn with an external expert. Just because we are all in the space at the same time doesn't mean we can't have personalization by connecting the ideas to our own practice.

## Cycles of Inquiry in Workshops

Consider this: When talking to an educator, what's the first thing that comes up in the teachers' lounge or at the dinner table? It's not the PD they attended. It's not the amazing math lesson they delivered. The first thing that teachers tend to talk about is kids. It could be a story about how they observed a moment where a kid just got it or, more often, it is about the kids that *aren't* getting it.

If you are facilitating a workshop, we suggest structuring the session as the beginning of a cycle of inquiry. The workshop would really be just the start of the learning, or the prelude to the learning. Let's consider how this could look using the Evolving Learner Cycle of Inquiry: Focus, Learn, Refine, Reflect.

TEACHING IS ALL ABOUT RESPONDING TO YOUR LEARNERS' NEEDS, AND PROFESSIONAL LEARNING SHOULD BE ABOUT RESPONDING TO TEACHERS' NEEDS.

Teaching is all about responding to your learners' needs, and professional learning should be about responding to teachers' needs. So, how do we find out what teachers' needs are before we plan the next workshop? Well, one way is to ask. To make professional learning relevant and meaningful, decision makers must ask teachers what they need in order to support their kids' learning. As we also discussed earlier, "choice" is one of Knowles's Four Principles of Andragogy. Yet, the *Teachers Know Best* report found that only 18 percent of teachers have voice and choice in their professional development.

18%
of teachers have voice and choice
in their professional development

Logistically, asking teachers what they need might seem a bit overwhelming and complicated, but really it depends on the professional learning experience. If the PL is at one school site, then the lead facilitator could attend a PLC beforehand and get curious about who (which kids) the teachers are talking about. If the PL is for a district, then a survey would be more appropriate. Possible questions to ask:

- Tell me about one student who is on your mind even after that child leaves the school. What is it about the student?

- What is one area where the student needs support—behavior, SEL, content-specific?

- What else would you like to say about this student?

Tip: Ask teachers to share stories, but make sure they do not include identifying information, to ensure the learner's privacy is protected.

### Focus: Identify the Needs

Once you have identified the learning needs (the *focus*), then start to plan your PL considering the following:

- How will the learning be connected to practice?
- How does our focus align with school/district goals?
- How can we leverage the knowledge in the room and build relationships?

As teachers, we want to be validated for our hard work, and what better way to do that than by utilizing our expertise during professional learning. The goal is to collaborate with our peers to solve POP through a cycle of inquiry. Staying problem-centered allows us to challenge each other in a way that is constructive. We all fear criticism, but professional learning should mirror the learning experiences we want for kids.

### Learn and Refine: Connecting

> "Connection is why we're here. We are hardwired to connect with others. It's what gives purpose and meaning to our lives, and without it, there is suffering."
>
> —Brené Brown

One thing we've learned in our experience both leading and participating in professional learning is that teachers want to feel connected. We know how lonely the job can be, so giving time to connect with peers to feel seen and heard is powerful. Knight (2016) says, "Everyone, adults and children, experiences greater well-being when they are heard, respected, and engaged" (p. 2). Whether you are doing face-to-face or online professional learning, we suggest starting PL with community building, and it is imperative that our conversations are driven by our *focus*. For example, what problem are we trying to solve in our cycle of inquiry? There will be temptation to vent, but this is a time to be curious and find solutions.

Try putting teachers into groups by similar student needs/challenges for these discussions. Talking best practices with fellow teachers can be just the thing they need. As the teachers are discussing, make sure to give them a brain break. We know the importance of brain breaks for our kids, so make sure to implement them for adult learners as well. This discussion time will allow teachers to *learn* strategies from their peers in order to *refine* their practice. The *refine* part will then happen in the classroom with the support of peers, leadership, and instructional coaches.

### Reflect: Restorative Practice Circle

End the PL with a time of *reflect*ion. Consider using a *restorative practice circle*. This can be as simple as having all the teachers stand in a circle. Make sure that everyone is able to be seen and heard. This means you'll have to make your circle bigger or smaller to accommodate this. Pose this sentence frame: I started the session feeling _____ and I am leaving feeling _____. Encourage them to only use one word to fill in each blank. This short activity will tell you a lot about where the teacher is. This is also a great way for kids to reflect and end their day. While we mention teachers specifically, this model would also work with principals. This would allow principals time to discuss POP at their school sites with other principals with similar POPs.

> "When teachers stop learning, so do students."
>
> —Jim Knight

In this section, we acknowledged the utility, as well as the shortcomings, of workshops. In the following sections, we introduce the two most utilized models of collaborative professional learning: professional learning communities and instructional coaching. Both models can build on workshops by offering powerful opportunities for teacher inquiry and refinement of instructional practices.

# PROFESSIONAL LEARNING COMMUNITIES (PLCS)

The term *professional learning communities* has a history dating back as far as the 1960s, but the concept didn't hit a tipping point until right before the turn of the century with the publication of *Professional Learning Communities at Work: Best Practices for Enhancing Student Achievement* by Richard DuFour and Robert Eaker (1998). According to DuFour, DuFour, Eaker, and Many (2006), the official definition of PLCs, found at allthingsplc.info/about, is the following:

> An ongoing process in which educators work collaboratively in recurring cycles of collective inquiry and action research to achieve better results for the students they serve. Professional learning communities operate under the assumption that the key to improved learning for students is continuous job-embedded learning for educators.

The term *professional learning communities*, or *PLCs*, is in a sense a name brand that has been widely adopted into education as a common term. However, you may hear other terms that are also in alignment with PLCs. For example, *learning teams* is used by Linda Darling-Hammond and others from the School Redesign Network at Stanford University, and in the Learning Forward standards, the term used is *learning communities*. In short, PLCs are about leveraging relationships with peers in a cycle of inquiry to improve our practice in order to improve learning for all kids.

PLCs, when done well, can be a compelling way for learning to happen from peers. At the very least, PLCs are a regularly scheduled meeting for school teams to come together and talk about kids. Richard Dufour (2004) states that there are three big ideas around PLCs: ensuring that kids learn, a culture of collaboration, and centering on results. The focus is on data surrounding academic, behavioral, and social success of kids, and it is important to note that when we say "data," we are referring to both quantitative and qualitative. In the current state of education, the term *data-driven* has become synonymous with quantitative test scores, but as educators, we know that one assessment will not tell a learner's story, which is why in Chapter 1, we highlighted a variety of options for gathering qualitative data (e.g., the Question Formulation Technique). According to the Learning Forward standards,

> Data from multiple sources enrich decisions about professional learning that leads to increased results for every student. Multiple sources include both quantitative and qualitative data, such as common formative and summative assessments, performance assessments, observations, work samples, performance metrics, portfolios, and self-reports. The use of multiple sources of data offers a balanced and more comprehensive analysis of student, educator, and system performance than any single type or source of data can. However, data alone do little to inform decision making and increase effectiveness.

PLCs depend on having conversations around the whole child, digging into strategies that have shown results and collaborating on ideas to improve learning.

Henry Blair Powell Elementary, a mid-size school with 80 percent or more of kids enrolled in free and reduced-price lunch, takes the idea of PLCs and the coaching cycle and has combined them into an *innovation cycle*. The idea is that teachers are continually innovating their practice to target kids' needs. In one particular meeting, a second-grade team was discussing the progress of their kids' reading. The team consisted of two veteran teachers, two new teachers, and an instructional coach. The instructional coach facilitates the conversations and captures the discussion on a document shared with the entire team. A team lead can also take the place of an instructional coach, but there is a benefit in having an outside person be in on the meetings because it adds a level of accountability along with another supportive person in the room to help with team dynamics. If funding is unavailable for an instructional coach, then it is essential to have a team lead who creates a safe space to share ideas. Looking at the three big ideas of PLCs, one thing that is assumed is trust. Teachers have to be able to trust each other to be vulnerable about their kids' learning, and they have to be willing to get past the idea of "my kids" and trust that it is the team's kids. Kids' success depends on how vulnerable a teacher is in regard to the kids' progress and how willing the teacher is to admit that there are other ways of learning that haven't been considered.

> **TEACHERS HAVE TO BE ABLE TO TRUST EACH OTHER TO BE VULNERABLE ABOUT THEIR KIDS' LEARNING, AND THEY HAVE TO BE WILLING TO GET PAST THE IDEA OF "MY KIDS" AND TRUST THAT IT IS THE TEAM'S KIDS.**

In the *innovation cycle*, teachers are utilizing the coaching cycle with innovation in mind. Let's look back at the second-grade team and their kids' progress with reading. First, the team sets a goal *(focus)*. The goal needs to be attainable and measurable in a time frame that is reasonable. Next, a team will go and teach, observe, and record data *(learn)*. The magic happens when the team comes back together to analyze the data and have a conversation *(refine)*. This conversation is a time of *reflect*ion and a time to *refine* practice. Consider the following example.

The second-grade team was having a great conversation about kids stuck at a specific reading level. The two veteran teachers were exchanging ideas and giving a background of their kids' needs. The two new teachers were sitting quietly. The instructional coach looked at the data of the two new teachers and realized their kids were stuck at a level a bit lower than those of the veteran teachers. The instructional coach then started asking the veteran teachers questions.

> *Instructional coach: Wow, veteran teachers, I'm noticing your data, and I am just curious how you were able to move all of your kids past this particular level.*

> *Veteran teachers: Oh, yeah, second-grade kids always struggle at that level. We have seen it for years. That's why we hit high-frequency words hard, and we send home these word lists so that the kids can work on them at home. They enjoy it because once they get one list down, then they get the next list.*

*Instructional coach: That's awesome. New teachers, have you seen these word lists? This can be a great strategy to try with these particular kids.*

The interesting part is that the veteran teachers were not intentionally withholding information, nor were the new teachers not asking for help. It just took looking at the data to truly realize that these two veteran teachers had a wealth of knowledge that seemed second nature to them. It also took a third party to ask the questions that are sometimes hard to ask as a first-year teacher. Jim Knight notes in *Better Conversations* (2016) the importance of communication and states that, "When trust, respect, and clear communication are cultural norms, teachers are more comfortable sharing ideas and learning from each other" (p. 3). Knight goes on to say, "the most important and powerful way we can improve our schools is to improve the way we interact with each other" (p. 3).

Now, let's be honest: PLCs are widely practiced, districts have adopted the PLC format, principals have found a time for PLCs to happen, norms are formed, but true PLCs are not always happening. Why is that? It seems as though there really isn't a clear understanding of what a PLC is. PLCs often turn into lesson planning and time to catch up about field trips and who's going to make copies for the week. Rarely are PLCs actually digging into data, and when they are, ego often gets in the way. So, how do you get around ego? Trust. Developing trust as the foundation for a PLC will allow teachers to open up about their kids, their ideas, and their strategies.

Once there is trust and a common understanding that feedback is to make us better, we are much more open to receiving it. The three of us even experienced this as we were writing this book. It was the very first meeting with our publisher, Dan, after we submitted our first piece of writing for review. We were anxious about the feedback, and we will never forget how the conversation started. Dan said, "Throughout this process, I would like you to think of me as a critical friend. I'm here to make your writing better." With every iteration of our writing, the content got markedly better. We needed Dan to challenge us in our own cycle of inquiry to write this book. The reality is that we all need what Adam Grant, an organizational psychologist and leading expert on work life, calls a "challenge network."

> "Along with a support network, we should all have a challenge network: a group of people who give us feedback and push us to improve."
>
> —Adam Grant
> twitter.com/adammgrant

The work we do with kids is important, and we need to challenge each other to do better. You may find that through your *peers* in a PLC, which we will be discussing further below; you may find it in your *kids;* and you may find it in *the world*. If you are like us, you will find your challenge network in all three.

## Reformatting PLCs

PLCs meet on a regular basis, typically once a week for less than an hour. In this very short time period, teachers arrive rushed, frustrated by a behavior issue, and then spend the first few minutes of the PLC venting about what the day has been like so far. So, how do we reformat PLCs? Logistically speaking, there are ways to make PLCs a trusting environment grounded in inquiry. Start every PLC with a mindfulness activity.

**MAKE PLCS A TRUSTING ENVIRONMENT GROUNDED IN INQUIRY. START EVERY PLC WITH A MINDFULNESS ACTIVITY.**

According to neuroscience, the brain needs to be in a calm state in order to learn and grow. Teachers running from one thing to the next need a moment to settle their mind and become present. Taking a moment to breathe or stretch creates a space for a more focused conversation. By modeling mindfulness during PLCs, teachers can then take this back to the students in order for them to see the importance of this calm state. Once the teachers have breathed and become present, start by looking at recent data and begin by *focusing* on one kid. By becoming curious about the data, teachers will begin to see trends in student learning. This is where teachers, as a team, *learn* strategies from each other to use with students. The conversation needs to stay focused on kids, and teachers need to be vulnerable in admitting that what they have tried so far is not working, and they need new ideas to help their students grow because our kids are worth that. Use a spreadsheet to take notes on the ideas and strategies that are being discussed. This data can then be used for interventions/student study team (SST) purposes. The next step would be for the teacher to go back to the classroom and *refine* practices with this student. For the next week, the teacher tries out the strategies and takes note if the student is improving. At the next PLC, the teachers *reflects* on whether or not the strategies worked and comes up with more strategies to try. This cycle will last about 6 weeks. Consider following Nancy Fichtman Dana and Diane Yendol-Hoppey's "Top Ten List: Essential Elements of a Healthy PLC," from *The PLC Book* (2015).

## HEALTHY PLCS DO THE FOLLOWING:

1. Establish a vision that creates momentum for their learning.
2. Build trust among group members.
3. Understand and embrace collaboration.
4. Encourage, recognize, and appreciate diversity within the group.
5. Promote the development of critical friends.
6. Pay attention to the work "in between" meetings.
7. Hold the group accountable for and document their learning.
8. Have a comprehensive view of what constitutes data and are willing to consider all forms and types of data throughout their PLC work.
9. Understand change and acknowledge the discomfort it may bring to some PLC members.
10. Work with their building administrators.

PLCs are more than just collaborating, and it is important to note that teachers that team well together might not be having an impact on student achievement. Elisa B. MacDonald (2013) discusses the hurdles involved in PLCs in *The Skillful Team Leader: A Resource for Overcoming Hurdles to Professional Learning for Student Achievement.* MacDonald addresses the hurdles by first identifying them and recognizing that all teams go through a life cycle together. Tuckman's (1965) model shows that teams move through five developmental stages: forming, storming, norming, performing, and adjourning (see figure to the right). Knowing the normalcy of these phases can help the team understand what is happening and can also be a tool for an instructional coach to support the team in whatever phase they are in.

| FORMING | STORMING | NORMING | PERFORMING | ADJOURNING |
|---|---|---|---|---|
| • Unclear purpose<br>• Superficial interactions, polite<br>• Lack of established trust<br>• Hesitant to share ideas and feedback<br>• Members dependent | • Unclear purpose or clear with varied interpretations<br>• Cliques, fight for position, mistrust<br>• Shutdown of ideas<br>• Resist feedback<br>• Members independent | • Shared purpose, shared understanding<br>• Agreed-upon approach to working together and solving conflict<br>• Initial trust<br>• Openness to ideas<br>• Welcome feedback<br>• Members interdependent | • Shared mission to achieve shared purpose<br>• High trust, high risk<br>• Seek alternate opinions and ideas<br>• Invite feedback<br>• Members interdependent<br>• Evidence of influencing student achievement | • Achieved shared purpose<br>• Team dispersed but learning and implementation are sustained<br>• Members interdependent |

*Source:* MacDonald, *The Skillful Team Leader* (Corwin, 2013). Adapted from Tuckman, B. W. (1965). Developmental Sequence in Small Groups. *Psychological Bulletin,* 63(6), 384–399.

## Principal PLCs

Ready to be let in on a little secret? *PLCs are not just for classroom teachers.* The process of examining data, inquiry, discussion, and mutual engagement is incredibly valuable for those in many school roles, including the principal. Nancy Fichtman Dana, Carol Thomas, and Sylvia Boynton (2011) describe a *principal professional learning community (PPLC)* as a small group that meets regularly "to learn from practice through structured dialogue and engagement in continuous cycles of inquiry" (p. 22). This inquiry can surround ideas, problems, improvement, passions, pitfalls, and more. Outside of the obvious benefits of sourcing solutions and ideas from other administrators, the primary—and arguably the most important—function of a PPLC can be summed up in one word: connection.

Much like teaching at times, the life of an administrator can be lonely and "historically plagued by isolation" (Dana et al., 2011, p. 25). Finding connection and acknowledgment in times of confusion, frustration, or adversity can be key in helping not only the administrator, but an entire school to thrive. In fact, leveraging the power of a PPLC as a group can help build community across school sites and end the idea of schools operating as individual silos. Sourcing the collective intelligence and experience of a group of administrators can be powerful, regardless of whether they face the same challenges. While it may seem like you would only want to be a part of a PPLC with schools that are similar to your own, consider this thought: Can teachers learn from other educators with dissimilar backgrounds, classrooms, grade levels, or challenges? Of course you would say yes. So wouldn't that translate to administrators as well?

*How* PPLCs are conducted is just as important as *why* they should take place. While it may seem simple to agree that principals should meet and participate in analysis and inquiry, the process of a traditional PLC often doesn't translate as well to administrators when they are operating as lead learners (Dana et al., 2011). For administrators who are used to thinking on their feet and quickly moving from problem to problem, "reflection, research and conversation about dilemmas can often feel uncomfortable and drawn out, almost antithetical to the harried pace at which they are used to working" (Dana et al., p. 30). This mode, however uncomfortable or initially awkward, helps to slow the pace and drive introspection, inquiry, and reflection. The accountability of these types of exercises is perhaps most necessary in the lonely administrator role, which further serves to bolster our need for the PPLC model.

*Blake, a fairly new elementary school principal, spent the better part of his first year in the role sifting through feelings of confusion, loneliness, inadequacy, and fear that he wasn't being as "impactful" a leader as he had always hoped he'd be. The real problem, however, proved to be that Blake really didn't have anyone to talk to about it. "I was floundering, for sure," Blake commented, "but honestly I just felt lost as to who I should talk to about it or get advice from." Teachers and other employees are hardly the sounding board for feelings of inadequacy when you are trying to be the "fearless leader." Blake also didn't want to chat with his boss or other superiors when he was confused and felt like perhaps his actions weren't having the desired effect. So when Blake's district started a pilot program of the PPLC model, Blake jumped on the opportunity. "It felt like this could really help me to learn from my colleagues and maybe even ease my anxieties about feeling like the only principal with issues," Blake shared. Blake was grouped with a heterogeneous group of four other administrators from a variety of backgrounds, school sites, and experience. Intimidation initially set in, but through conversation and regular meetings, Blake remarked, "I really started to feel at ease and that I could ask and share in a safe space." More than that, Blake and his group began to gain benefits from examining data and asking the hard questions. Blake acknowledged that the pace at times felt slow and different, but that the group agreed that it yielded the best results through conversation and questions. Blake concluded, "Honestly, the PPLC model is what helped boost my confidence and drive me forward, feeling supported rather than floating around alone."*

Connection, conversation, structure, and inquiry are key elements for successful educators, and also successful administrators. *Learning from peers* extends far beyond the classroom and helps administrators not only model professional learning, but also reap the continual benefits.

Now that we've discussed PLCs, PLCs with coaching, and PLCs for principals, we need to dive deeper into what the role of an instructional coach involves. Whether your site has a full-time teacher dedicated to instructional coaching or this role has been unofficially filled by other educators/leaders, the time spent collaborating can be optimized by knowing the essentials such as how to build and maintain relationships. As much as we support instructional coaching, we must emphasize that coaching is not for everyone, and it is important to roll out coaching as something that is a strategy for learning and not something that is mandatory. As Knight (2018) notes, principals may "damage coaching relationships before the coaching even begins. When teachers are told they have no choice but to participate in coaching, they may be inclined to see coaching as a punishment more than a support and, therefore, resist" (p. 159). Again, we stick to Knowles's principles of adult learning—in particular, *choice* remains a main factor in the implementing of instructional coaching.

> "Coaching is a form of professional development that brings out the best in people, uncovers strengths and skills, builds effective teams, cultivates compassion, and builds emotionally resilient educators. Coaching at its essence is the way that human beings, and individuals, have always learned best."
> —Elena Aguilar

Jim Knight (2018), author and known authority on this topic, provides the following definition: "Instructional coaches partner with teachers to analyze current reality, set goals, identify and explain teaching strategies to hit the goals, and provide support until the goals are met" (p. 22). Similar to PLCs, instructional coaching is about a cycle of inquiry, and the two are not mutually exclusive. It is not uncommon to see a school practicing PLCs with the support of an instructional coach.

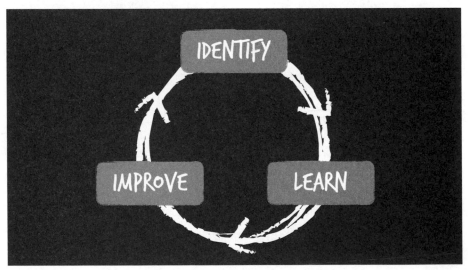

### Impact Cycle

Jim Knight's cycle of inquiry for professional learning starts with "Identify," where the teacher examines current realities of one's practice by reviewing observation data, student interviews, or student work, or by watching a video of one's teaching. Ideally, multiple data points are analyzed. (Note: The power of video for analyzing your own practice cannot be overstated, and we will discuss this later in the chapter.) The instructional coach facilitates the process by asking the "identify questions," and the partnership leads to the teacher identifying a student-focused goal. In the "Learn" step, the partnership continues as the coach shares teaching strategies that are aligned with the teacher's student-focused goal. The teacher chooses an approach to observe in practice, and the coach models it. "Improve" involves the teacher implementing the practice as well as the coach and teacher gathering data and evaluating the progress toward the student-focused goal. This step also involves iterating until the goal is met.

## COACHING PRINCIPLES AND PRACTICES

A coaching cycle, like any other cycle of inquiry will require the essential elements included in the Evolving Learner Cycle of Inquiry: Focus, Learn, Refine, Reflect. However, to give specific context, the *focus* of a coaching cycle often involves a pre-observation meeting between the coach and teacher learner where a goal is set. In other words, what are we looking to improve? The pre-observation meeting also moves into the *learn* part of an inquiry cycle as the coach and teacher learner discuss (and possibly research) strategies to reach that goal. Next is the implementation, which usually involves a classroom observation, but it could also be accomplished with a video recording of the lesson being implemented. We call this step "refine" because even in the moments of instruction, we as educators are using formative assessment to adjust our instructional moves, but this is also an opportunity to *learn*. After implementation is the debrief or *reflect* stage where the coach and teacher learner think about what worked, what didn't, and how this professional learning experience can be applied to other areas of teaching and learning. As we mentioned in Chapter 1, in inquiry-based learning cycles, we often move back and forth between parts of the cycle, as learning is messy and rarely fits into a perfectly linear process. It is also important to note that the cycle never really ends. Rather, we decide if we still need to iterate on a particular skill or find a new *focus*.

Instructional coaches provide a safe place for teachers to take risks and fail with a safety net in the room with them. This safety net allows teachers to feel supported to try new things. Instructional coaches are that extra body in the room that is there if the teacher needs them. Most of the time, they don't, but it sure does feel nice to have someone just in case. In fact, research from Joyce and Showers (1995, 2002) shows the vast difference in the implementation of new practices when there is research, theory, demonstrations, and practice with coaching/mentoring. Without coaching/mentoring, there is only a five to ten percent chance of a teacher's new skills/knowledge transferring into the classroom. With coaching/mentoring, the percentage jumps to 80 to 90.

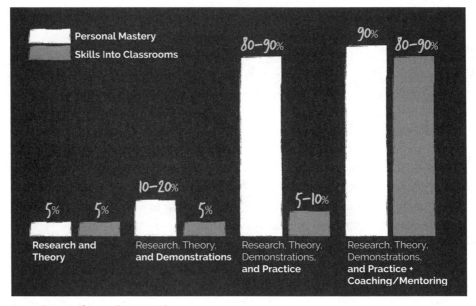

*Source:* Joyce & Showers (1995, 2002)

More and more, schools and districts are going to one-to-one devices for kids. These initiatives are expensive and require the teachers to be the ones to implement the technology. The problem is that many schools and districts only put aside money for the devices and the infrastructure needed to utilize these devices like Wi-Fi access points or an increase in IT to support the technology. It is critical to plan for the total cost of ownership, which includes budgeting money to support teachers in adopting new instructional strategies. We have heard heartbreaking stories of the waste and missed opportunities this leads to. A principal at a school confided in us that a schoolwide initiative provided devices for *all* kids, but halfway through the school year they realized that one team of teachers had yet to let the kids use the devices. For 5 months, these devices collected dust when they could have been personalizing learning and making a real difference for kids who were struggling or were bored.

The instructional coach was pulled in to support the team and found that the teachers were apprehensive and didn't know what to ask for in regard to how to use the device. They didn't even know where to start. By spending an afternoon with the team in a cycle of inquiry, the coach led the group in analyzing the situation and developing a plan for how the devices could address the needs of learners. That same day, IT was able to install applications to the device, and the teachers were ready to start implementing teaching and learning with the devices the very next day. The coach was able to touch back a few more times to evaluate how the teachers were doing, and to the coach's delight, the teachers were thriving and using the devices more than most of the grade levels and, more importantly, the use of the devices was improving teaching and learning.

The teachers at this site were fortunate to have an instructional coach with the knowledge, skills, and dispositions to quickly build a relationship and guide them through a cycle of inquiry, but the reality is that even the most seasoned teacher of children needs to acquire new knowledge, skills, and (possibly) dispositions to work shoulder to shoulder with other educators. As we will discuss further below, Dr. Christine Olmstead, Associate Superintendent of Educational Services at Orange County (California) Department of Education (OCDE), identified a need for schools and districts to personalize professional learning for instructional coaches that was competency-based, effective, and scalable. In other words, exceptional teachers of children are entering the role of instructional coaches, but they need professional learning opportunities to coach adults. To research the competencies that needed to be included in these micro-credentials, OCDE contracted with the nonpartisan, nonprofit research, development, and service agency, WestEd. These are the competencies that have been identified for instructional coaches:

1. Building and maintaining a relationship with teacher learner
2. Effective communication
3. The coaching process
4. Gathering objective evidence and the feedback process
5. Matching coaching supports to teacher learner
6. Cycle of improving teaching and learning

If you are interested in a deep dive on the topic of instructional coaching, we will share a list of resources at the end of this section. Moving forward, we want to explore some innovative approaches to instructional coaching.

## Video Coaching

A common practice for instructional coaches is to spend time in a teacher's room for an observation of a lesson, and then to give the teacher feedback at a later time following the observation. The issue with this is that the teacher is unable to see what the instructional coach saw, not to mention the fact that it is difficult to receive feedback because of the shame factor and the vulnerability it takes to allow someone to come in and watch them teach. One school district we have worked with started using video feedback in their beginning teacher induction program. First- and second-year teachers are timid about feedback. They know they are new at teaching, so they know they are struggling on a daily basis. It is important for them to feel the love and not feel a sense of shame in response to feedback. By utilizing video software, instructional coaches are able to record a lesson (they actually do not even need to be in the room) and then pause throughout the video and insert feedback. For new teachers, much of this feedback needs to be affirming and specific. Affirming feedback will build collective efficacy and will allow them to be open to feedback that will help them improve. An instructional coach using this tool can add questions throughout the video in order for the teacher to spend time reflecting. The teacher is able to see herself or himself teaching and will notice more through this time of self-reflection. Ideally, this method instills reflection and allows for self-actualization, two skills that are vital for educators. It's important to note that not everybody has access to video coaching software, but we feel that the easy access to video technology with smartphones and tablets has really revolutionized the field.

## Coaching Coaches With Micro-Credentials

We've referenced our own Evolving Learning Cycle of Inquiry, but there are other design models such as the 5 E's referenced in Chapter 1 and the ADDIE model illustrated below.

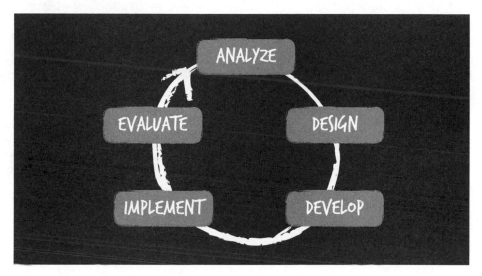

*Source:* Adapted from instructional design materials developed by the Center for Educational Technology at Florida State University

I, Lainie, first came to know the ADDIE model through my work with BloomBoard when I was asked to lead an OCDE pilot of micro-credentials designed for instructional coaches. The purpose of the pilot was to find a way to personalize professional learning for instructional coaches that was competency-based, effective, and scalable. We were seeing exceptional teachers enter the role of instructional coaches, those who had demonstrated their effectiveness as teachers of children but may not have had any experience teaching adults, and they may be the only instructional coach in their school, district, or region. A one-time workshop would not meet the need. Who was going to coach the coaches? How would we ensure that they had the knowledge, skills, and dispositions to be effective instructional coaches? The answer was micro-credentials, and we asked Jason Lange, entrepreneur and cofounder of BloomBoard, to explain the process.

*How does the micro-credentials process improve teaching and learning through a cycle of inquiry?*

When implemented effectively, micro-credentials are really a unique combination of the following:

1.  Portfolio-based learning (for which there's a lot of emerging research showing substantial gains in learning and retention at much faster rates)

2.  A cycle of inquiry in which participants are asked to *analyze* an existing competency, *design* and/or *develop* an intervention based on that analysis, *implement* the intervention and capture the necessary portfolio of evidence, and then *evaluate* one's success in good reflective practice (Again, there's a *ton* of research on the efficacy of cycles of inquiry to drive change in practice and improve effective instruction.)

3.  A collaborative, peer-driven feedback process designed to enable participants working on the same competency to give and receive feedback on their portfolios of demonstrated practice. These three components create the ideal conditions for "productive struggle" necessary for meaningful learning at any age.

Now that we've covered the two major categories of collaborative models of professional learning, PLCs and coaching, we turn our attention to some practical ways to learn from peers. Hopefully, this section can be a place where you can grab ideas for your educational setting. Behind each idea, the intention is that teachers are connecting to their purpose and what they value. By learning from each other, teachers can feel connected, seen, and heard. The hope is really that this connection would then overflow into the classroom so that kids can feel connected, seen, and heard.

# PRACTICES IN ACTION: FEELING CONNECTED, SEEN, AND HEARD

> "Shame unravels our connection to others. In fact, I often refer to shame as the fear of disconnection—the fear of being perceived as flawed and unworthy of acceptance or belonging."
>
> —Brené Brown

Collaboration, creativity, critical thinking, and communication are known as the four Cs of 21st-century learning. If sharing ideas and collaborating are what makes us better, than what holds us back from sharing? As a first-year teacher, and maybe even as a veteran teacher, there is this feeling that if we don't know, then how can we be teachers? Teachers are supposed to be experts, right? Or, are teachers supposed to be models of the idea that it's okay not to know. So, then, what holds us back? Brené Brown, a shame researcher, describes shame as the fear of disconnection—fear of being flawed. It seems that shame might be one possibility of what is holding us back from being vulnerable and admitting that we don't know everything. What's even more upsetting is that if you ask teachers, they will tell you that they want kids to feel safe to fail, to ask questions, and to admit to not knowing something because we are dying to teach them what they don't know. How can we expect our kids to do this if we aren't modeling it ourselves?

> "In order for connection to happen, we have to allow ourselves to be seen—really seen."
>
> —Brené Brown

Vulnerability is the prerequisite for learning from peers. For peers to learn from each other, there has to be a connection there, a vulnerability, and allowance to be seen by someone else. This takes risk—risking that an idea might be rejected, might not be valued, might not be heard.

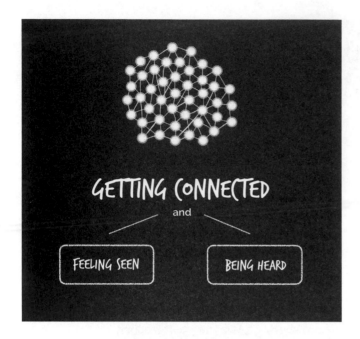

GETTING CONNECTED

and

FEELING SEEN     BEING HEARD

## Getting Connected

Building trust with teachers and students helps to develop a partnership that will turn into deeper learning. In *Culturally Responsive Teaching and the Brain: Promoting Authentic Engagement and Rigor Among Culturally and Linguistically Diverse Students,* Zaretta Hammond (2015) defines this as learning partnerships and describes the importance of a social-emotional partnership because our brains are wired for connection. By creating a connection that is authentic, giving feedback, and holding each other to high standards, teachers can build capacity. *Learning partnership* is one of four areas that are important for being a culturally responsive teacher. The others are *awareness, information processing, and community building.* Create learning partnerships as a team, or find someone on your staff that is willing to partner with you.

*Book Clubs*

What better way to spark conversations and learning between peers than around a book club reading? Book clubs are a great way for teachers to learn the material and then share out their insights together. When diving into the Evolving Learner Cycle, book clubs would be a great resource to introduce as a resource in the learn stage. Teachers (or the school/district) might identify a goal to focus on for the year, so a book club can be done all year long for the whole site or done with a team during PLC.

Pressed for time? Offer book clubs over the summer. Teachers can get together to discuss in person, or they can post their learning on social media with the district's hashtag. This takes the pressure off of having to meet up. It also serves as a reminder for those that haven't participated in the book club and allows them to access the information. Book clubs provide a way for teachers to feel connected to the work and to each other.

*Take Breaks*

Take the time to take a break (recess, lunch), whatever that looks like during your day. The reason for this is for you. Siegel (2010; Siegel & Bryson, 2012) explains how the brain is wired for "we" and discusses the importance of having time to build connections. Take the time to interact with your peers. A lot of learning can happen during breaks—and a lot of refreshment is needed to keep going and refuel.

## Feel Seen

The boom of social media has allowed our world to be more connected than ever. Hashtags are a way to filter information so that it is visible and seen, making it searchable and discoverable for anyone. Schools have capitalized on this by creating school hashtags or even district hashtags. This is a public hashtag that can be viewed by anyone and is a way for everyone to celebrate what the school district or school is doing. From this hashtag, teachers are *seeing* what other teachers are doing, and they can then reach out to ask questions so they can use the idea in their own classrooms. Teachers have also been able to set up observations at other sites from something they saw on social media. Professional learning opportunities have been developed based on a teacher posting something she or he is doing in the classroom. Utilizing social media gives teachers the freedom to learn on their own time, to see others, and to be seen. There are lots of ways to learn from hashtags that we go deeper into in Chapter 3, "Learning From the World."

Feeling *seen* also happens by sharing our practice with peers around us, in our school/district. We believe that some of the best professional learning comes from seeing each other in practice, and *instructional rounds* is a set of protocols and processes designed to make that happen, focusing not only on instructional practices, but also on schoolwide improvement. The protocols and processes, an adaptation and extension of medical rounds, involve observing, analyzing, discussing, and understanding instruction. (City, Elmore, Fiarman, Teitel, & Lachman, 2018). While a schoolwide adoption of this network approach to improving teaching and learning is ideal, individual teachers can self-organize their own rounds to get feedback from their peers on specific teaching practices.

## Be Heard

### Podcasts

Podcasts are an outlet for educators to be heard. Each week, a group of staff members (teachers, secretaries, paraeducators, custodians, librarians, principals, and so forth) gets together and records a conversation. Each interview-styled podcast can be anywhere from 5 to 10 minutes (to an hour for longer subjects) and is published at the same time every week. Podcasts give educators a voice that is heard across their district and beyond. They do not take much to set up and record. The best part is that they are something you can listen to in the car, while you work out, or in the background while making dinner. There are also a lot of great podcasts for kids that can be used in the classroom or with your own child. Check out our end-of-chapter resources for some suggested podcasts to start with.

### Restorative Practices

According to Ted Wachtel, founder of the International Institute for Restorative Practices, "The fundamental premise of restorative practices is that people are happier, more cooperative and productive, and more likely to make positive changes when those in authority do things WITH them, rather than TO them or FOR them" (IIRP Staff, 2018). The framework for *restorative practices* includes a disciplinary approach to wrongdoing, but the focus is on building healthy relationships in a prevention/intervention approach to develop a positive school climate and culture. Restorative practices are often used with students, but they are so powerful that they translate perfectly to use with school staff members.

Giving time for restorative practices as a staff will allow everyone to feel heard. For you as a leader, restorative practices will give a true pulse as to what is going on with your staff and allow you to build a stronger school culture.

## Renovating Professional Learning

*Source:* unsplash.com/@nolanissac

Let's take a moment to think back on adult learning theory (recall Knowles's Four Principles from earlier in the chapter). The emphasis on adult learning theory is a reminder for professional learning designers that it is important to take these concepts into account as you plan and design the learning. For those of you on the receiving end of mandated professional learning, consider whether adult learning theory was taken into account. The next time you fill out a feedback form, talk about adult learning theory, and offer suggestions as to why you were unable to connect with the learning. Below are some ideas for implementing a renovated professional learning experience.

### Network Meetings

Teachers need time and space to learn from each other. One way this can happen is by having network meetings. These are a great place for teachers to meet each other and connect to socially construct knowledge. It is tempting to throw other learning into this meeting, but the key here is networking. Give teachers, or principals, time to chat, ask each other questions, and collaborate.

### Master Classes

Often the PD is a one-off session based on a textbook or concept. One way to change this up is to give teachers professional learning on one consistent idea throughout the year. At the beginning of the year, teachers are to pick from a choice of about 10 to 12 sessions. The range of choices offered are connected to district (and perhaps building or team-level) goals and objectives. Teachers pick the class they are interested in and then attend three after-school classes where they can collaborate and connect with teachers in the school district. The classes are taught by instructional coaches, teachers on special assignment, or teacher leaders in the district. The sessions last for about an hour. Within that hour, the PL provides a time to build community, self-assess where teachers are in the concept, learn more about the idea, give brain breaks, and end with a time of reflection.

### Day of Innovation

At the start of the school year, give teachers a day to innovate. This idea comes from Google's 20 percent project, where Google provides its employees 20 percent of their time to work on something they are passionate about. A day of innovation is a day for teachers to pick something they are passionate about and learn about it. It's as simple as that. Teachers can go on field trips, work alone, work together, plan, prep—whatever they need to innovate their classroom for the year. Offering a day of innovation tells the teachers that they are innovative, they are creative, and what they are passionate about has value. Ask teachers to share on social media how they innovated that day. Have them tell their story. Continue the work throughout the year by providing time for teachers to continue to innovate their practice. Adult learners need choice in topics as well as flexibility in things like where and how they learn.

### JOT (Just One Thing)

Highlight what teachers are doing by having them share at lunch or a staff meeting. JOTs are a quick, 15-minute share that allows teachers to demonstrate one thing they have been doing in their classroom. This can be a technology resource or lesson a teacher has tried out and wanted to share with peers. Some of the best teacher learning happens from seeing the successful practices of their peers.

"In the majority of schools, what's needed isn't more professional development on deconstructing standards or academic discourse or using data to drive instruction. What's needed is time, space, and attention to managing stress and cultivating resilience."

—Elena Aguilar

## SOCIAL-EMOTIONAL LEARNING

The Collaborative for Academic, Social, and Emotional Learning (CASEL) defines *social-emotional learning (SEL)* as a process that kids and adults go through in order to understand and manage emotions. CASEL splits this up into five core competencies: self-awareness, self-management, responsible decision making, relationship skills, and social awareness (casel.org/what-is-sel/). We are compelled to include SEL in this book because we really believe that explicitly teaching SEL to our kids is so important, and we have to remember that in order to truly teach it, we have to model it. That means it is important for us to understand the competencies so that we can genuinely live them out in front of our kids and our peers.

WE ARE COMPELLED TO INCLUDE SEL IN THIS BOOK BECAUSE WE REALLY BELIEVE THAT EXPLICITLY TEACHING SEL TO OUR KIDS IS SO IMPORTANT, AND WE HAVE TO REMEMBER THAT IN ORDER TO TRULY TEACH IT, WE HAVE TO MODEL IT.

The more we develop our own SEL capacity, the better equipped we are to collaborate in a climate of trust, mutual respect, and honesty. Relationships are the foundation for learning from peers and are often what gets in the way of learning from each other. Recognizing and growing in our own SEL allow us to have genuine connections with our peers, which will allow us to have better relationships, and that is better for all involved. The following are easy ways to build capacity in SEL.

## Mindfulness

Mindfulness is being aware of our thoughts, our reactions, our emotions, and our physical state. By being mindful, we are able to take a moment to understand the situation in front of us. Here are some ways to practice mindfulness:

### Calm Jars

Grab a mason jar (or a water bottle—even the little 8 oz bottles will work great), and fill it a quarter of the way with glitter. Fill the rest of the bottle with water. Place the lid back on and shake! Keep this jar on your desk for anyone (kids, peers) to shake. The idea is that we all need clarity in order to think. When our brains are not being mindful, they look like a glitter jar being shaken around, but the second we stop and take a breath, the glitter seems to settle, causing the jar to be clear (or our brains for that matter). This sense of clarity happens when we take a breath or a moment to be mindful.

### 5–2–5 Breathing

Never underestimate the power of a breath, especially when working with kids and adults. Take a deep breath in for 5 seconds, hold it for 2, and then breathe out deeply for 5 seconds. Repeat. Taking a deep breath like this allows us to create a sustained calm and lowers anxiety.

### The Story I'm Making Up

In *Dare to Lead,* Brené Brown (2018) discusses how to be a brave leader. The book is split into four parts: Rumbling With Vulnerability, Living Into Our Values, Braving Trust, and Learning to Rise. Each part really narrows in on what it means to be a leader and how vulnerability is such a huge part of that. In Part Four, Learning to Rise, Brown talks about how, "in the absence of data, we will always make up stories." Brown states that, "we are neurobiologically hard-wired to make sense of our hurt," so we quickly make up a story to justify how we are feeling (p. 258). We see this happening in education constantly because we are working with people (peers, kids, parents), and we let our emotions create a story in our head. We are convinced that a student isn't trying, or is being lazy even. We are convinced that a parent is out to get us. We are convinced that the teacher next door is trying to outdo us. Whatever the story may be, we let our minds go wild and instead of naming the feeling we are having, we let the story take over. This narrative that we make up in our head causes such division and distrust, and it can destroy a school community. A way to combat this is to get curious about how you are feeling, and then—this next step takes vulnerability—have a conversation with the person who is prompting you to create the story. By telling someone, "The story I am making up in my head is . . ." we are able to create a conversation that takes the issue and makes it into a separate thing. Often, the story we are making up is not even close to what the other person is thinking. We see this all the time with our kids who think that someone is staring at them, so they are staring at the person, and in return, the other person thinks he or she is being stared at too. It becomes a vicious cycle and can affect the way the two people interact from that day on. By naming the story, we are able to test if it is really true or not.

### Identify Feelings

Along with naming our narratives that we make up in our head, it is also important to pause and get curious about the emotions we are feeling. Kids—and, let's be honest, even adults—have a hard time with identifying emotions, and it is really important to explicitly teach how to identify our feelings. With kids, the bursts of anger tend to be called tantrums, but with adults we see the same kind of burst of anger from burying deep emotions that will all of a sudden explode. Brown calls this "chandeliering" because it is as if some sort of trigger pushes the person to rage straight up to the chandelier. Spending a moment to say, "I am feeling _____ because _____," helps us to identify the feeling and the "why" behind it. By simply identifying the feeling and acknowledging it, we are able to give it a name and understand why we are suddenly having strong emotions.

## Zones of Regulation

The *Zones of Regulation,* developed by Leah Kuypers (zonesofregulation.com/index.html), are a framework to foster self-regulation and emotional control.

The zones, split up into four colors—red, yellow, green, and blue—help us to recognize and communicate emotions and provide for a common language in discussing these feelings. Yes, the Zones of Regulation are meant for the classroom, but as we've seen, adults are not always the best at identifying their feelings either. Imagine being in a staff meeting or a PLC and being able to safely say, "I am in the red zone." Kuypers defines the zones as follows:

> Red zone: extremely heightened state with intense emotions like anger, rage, explosive behavior, devastation or terror

> Yellow zone: heightened state of alertness with elevated emotions with slightly more control than in the red zone. The feelings in this zone are stress, frustration, anxiety, excitement, silliness, or nervousness.

> Green zone: calm state of alertness with emotions that are happy, focused, content, ready to learn. This is the ideal zone to be in when learning.

> Blue zone: low state of alertness with emotions that are sad, tired, sick, or bored

The zones create a common language around the identification of emotions, and they also give a starting point for what to do when we are in the zone. Say we are in the red zone. First, we identify we are in the red zone, and then we can draw on strategies for getting us to the green zone.

Strategies by zone:

- Red zone: Take a deep breath, count to ten, walk away, take a break
- Yellow zone: Take a break, take a walk, take a deep breath, talk to my inner-self
- Green zone: Listen, focus, learn
- Blue zone: Take a deep breath, talk to an adult, think positive thoughts (Kuypers & Winner, 2017)

# TAKING CARE OF YOU

## BRAIN BREAKS

SHORT BURSTS OF MOVEMENT THAT HELP INCREASE BLOOD
FLOW AND SEND US OXYGEN TO OUR BRAIN.

## AFFIRMATIONS

TELL SOMEONE THAT YOU SEE THEM AND THAT YOU CARE.

## CALM CALENDAR

EACH DAY IN THE SCHEDULE INCLUDES A WAY TO BE CALM FOR THE DAY SO
THAT EVERYONE CAN THRIVE.

## PLAY

IF YOU ARE READING THIS, THEN TAKE A MOMENT TO PLAY. TAKE THE TIME TO
PLAY WITH YOUR STUDENTS, YOUR COLLEAGUES, AND YOUR OWN KIDS.

## Brain Breaks

Never underestimate the power of a brain break. Brain breaks are short bursts of movement that help increase blood flow and send oxygen to our brain. Brain breaks are great for our kids and for ourselves, so take them with your students. Imagine a staff meeting or a professional learning event that started with a brain break! How different our mental state would be if we had a moment to get our brain onboard. Examples of brain breaks are all over the internet. The most important thing is to get your body moving and to include cross-lateral movement so that both sides of your brain can wake up. This will help with that sleepy state that comes over us when we are sitting for long periods of time.

## Empathy

Brené Brown created a phenomenal video on the difference between empathy and sympathy (The RSA, 2013). Empathy can sometimes be confused with sympathy, but the truth is that the two are very different. In the video, Brown states that empathy "fuels connection" and that sympathy "drives disconnection." Brown goes on to say that "empathy is feeling with people." Empathy is so important in learning from peers because it allows us to connect with others on a deeper level, and when we are connected, we can learn from each other on this deeper level. Many feel that empathy is something that you either have or don't have, but it truly can be taught. By using reflective listening, we can all grow more in our empathy.

## Affirmations

One meaning of *affirmation* is an acknowledgment of someone with words or actions. By giving someone an affirmation, you are telling that person, I see you and I care. We have all worked with someone who isn't easy to work with. Consider leaving the person an affirmation note along with that person's favorite snack or coffee. A little act of kindness goes a long way. We have no idea where other people are in their journey, but we do know that we can be kind and care about them. Affirmations help to build trust and rapport, but it may take some time. Small interactions that are positive and consistent will really help to nurture that trust relationship. Be disciplined in giving affirmations. Try doing one at the same time every day. Not only will this make the other person feel amazing, but it will also make you feel great and get your mind off any negative feelings.

## Social Thinking

*Social Thinking* is a social skills curriculum developed by Michelle Garcia Winner (socialthinking.com). The mission of Social Thinking is "to help people develop their social competencies to better connect with others and live happier, more meaningful lives." This curriculum gives teachers and students a common language to use when socializing. Students (and adults) benefit from being explicitly taught how to socialize with one another. This is something we can all continue to grow in. In education, there has been a high emphasis on assessments. Social Thinking is a way for educators to get back to teaching each other how to interact as humans.

## Calm Calendar

Most schools have some sort of schedule that goes out to the staff to help keep the week organized. One way to make this even more streamlined is by creating this schedule in an online collaborative space (e.g., Google Docs) that can be edited throughout the week because, let's be honest, schedules change. On this calendar, consider adding one professional learning article a week. This is a great way for us to grow in our practice. Even if we read just the title of the article, we will be thinking and processing the topic throughout the week.

Consider also including a "calm calendar" on the newsletter. Each day in the schedule, include a way to be calm for the day so that everyone can thrive. Take a look at the example below that was inspired by the Calm app:

| |
|---|
| **Monday:** Share a high, a low, and something that made you laugh from your year so far on social media. |
| **Tuesday:** Get outside and take a picture—a class selfie, perhaps? |
| **Wednesday:** Try a body scan. You can do this one with your students. |
| **Thursday:** Add one thing to, or take one thing away from, your classroom to make it more calming. Consider a calm corner for your students. |
| **Friday:** Notice where in your body you hold your tension. Invite it to soften. Sometimes your body just wants you to notice it. See if anything shifts during the day as a result. |

## Play

That's right, play. Play is not something that should be taken lightly. According to the American Academy of Pediatrics' recent report, *The Power of Play,* play can improve "executive functioning, language, early math skills (numerosity and spatial concepts), social development, peer relations, physical development and health, and [provide] an enhanced sense of agency" (pediatrics.aap publications.org/content/142/3/e20182058). If you look at trends of what type of presentation is most popular at education conferences, you will often find "hands-on" high up in the ranks because we as educators like to experience the learning (one of the four principles of adult learning theory). We like to play! In fact, Mitchel Resnick, author of *Lifelong Kindergarten: Cultivating Creativity Through Projects, Passion, Peers, and Play* (2017), states that kindergarten is the best invention in the past thousand years. Kindergarten was first thought up by Friedrich Froebel in Germany in 1837. He studied the classroom and noticed the "sit-and-get" format. He decided to shift the model to one that is more interactive where kids could play and interact. The need for this type of model does not go away after kindergarten, and it does not go away when we become adults either. Knowing the importance of play and how much we can learn from each other during play is why we thought it was important to mention it here. We hope that if you are reading this, you'll take a moment to play. Take the time to play with your students, your colleagues, and your own kids. For more ideas on play, look into *Purposeful Play: A Teacher's Guide to Igniting Deep and Joyful Learning Across the Day* by Kristine Mraz, Alison Porcelli, and Cheryl Tyler (2016). This book is divided into three sections: "All About Play," "The Work in Play," and "The Play in Work." The first section really emphasizes the reasons for play, in case you were still questioning the why, and it describes the developmental stages of play and how to move toward more mature play. As a side note, this is a wonderful book for anyone who is supervising recess and a great resource for educating parents on why play is so important.

## PARENTS/FAMILIES AS PEERS

Last, but definitely not least, we would be remiss if we didn't include our kids' parents/families in this chapter on peers. Just as our kids are often an underutilized resource, so are their parents/families. They are, without question, our *peers.* If you are raising a child, you are that child's first and constant teacher—plus, your job does not end in May or June.

Many of us wear both hats, parent and educator. We know the joys and challenges of teaching kids, and we know the joys and challenges of raising kids. Being an educator and a parent makes us unique. We know both worlds while most parents/families stopped experiencing the education system when they graduated from high school or college. Many have never been rostered groups of kids that they need to keep safe and educate for 6 hours a day, 5 days a week. Some parents/family members may have had negative experiences in their own education, which can make a school campus an uncomfortable place to be and educators intimidating to talk to, so they may avoid interactions. Some parents or family members, for a variety of reasons, fear that they are being left out of their child's education and school life. There is an unspoken power dynamic where parents/families can feel that they have little or no control over their child's education. After all, most parents/families rarely have a say in anything that happens at school, let alone the things we impose on their kids such as homework and projects. We need to go out of our way to make parents/families feel welcome and like valued members of the learning community. We also need to assume positive intent, even when it is difficult.

Thinking back to the term *scenius,* the parents and families raising the kids in our class have their own unique gifts (knowledge, skills, and dispositions), and we should get to know them and leverage them. Otherwise, you might have talent and expertise in your learning community and not knowing about it, that resource goes untapped. Furthermore, in your cycle of inquiry for professional learning, once you have identified your *focus* (e.g., problem of practice), consider the ways in which parents/families could be part of your *learn*ing to design a solution. For example, if my POP is that learners are not using credible sources when researching for projects at home, I need to investigate to see if I'm providing enough support for that. I can make assumptions, but I am much better off reaching out to parents/families and asking for their perspective. It is interesting that when we explore these problems, we might uncover that there is another problem in play. For example, maybe homework is infringing on family time and other after-school commitments, so kids are rushing their research. Involving parents/families as partners in our cycle of inquiry, we can design a solution that meets the needs of learners and removes a point of friction between home and school. We are all on the same team, striving to improve for the sake of our kids.

## TIPS: LISTEN, BE FLEXIBLE, CARE

### Leadership

**Listen:** Your coach can be a powerful tool in making change at your site. Coaches want to bring your vision to life. Listen to them as they share how things are going. The more communication between the administrator and the coach, the better the coaching will go.

**Be flexible:** You might have high expectations for how much growth you want to see happen at your site with your teachers. Remember that teachers are like students: They all grow at different rates. A teacher who may seem to be moving slowly all year might surge at the end of the year and be right where you want that teacher to be. Trust the process, and trust your coach.

**Care:** Care for your coaches. They are working tirelessly for you, for the teachers, and for the students. Coaches sometimes get overlooked. Make a point of *seeing* them.

### Instructional Coaches

**Listen:** Not saying anything can be the best thing you can do as a coach. When going in to meet with a coachee, let the teacher learner start the conversation. Teachers will tend to open with what's going on, and then you'll be able to hear what they really need in that moment. Be in tune with how the year is going and what time of year it is. Different seasons of the year cause different stressors. Build relationships from the start as someone teachers can come to when they need support. This will transfer later when you are discussing pedagogy.

**Be flexible:** You might have a goal for your teacher, but that might not be the same goal that the teacher wants to work on. It is important for the teacher to pick the goal (choice) because then the teacher will be more likely to work at it.

**Care:** Sometimes teachers just need a note of encouragement or even a coffee. This goes a long way. If you feel like a teacher is not moving forward, stop and bring the person a treat. We can't even express to you the power of a latte. If they know you care and that you are there for them, teachers will learn they can trust you and can keep going, keep persisting, and not burn out, regardless of the time of year.

## Classroom Teachers

**Listen:** Having a coach can make you feel very vulnerable. That's okay. You are going to come out the other end more confident and more in love with teaching. Listen to your coach, and be open to what your peer is saying. Your coach wants to see you shine.

**Be flexible:** Coaching is relational, so if a coach runs late because of being in someone else's room, don't sweat it. Your coach is trying to support everyone, including you.

**Care:** A teacher–coach relationship can be very powerful. Many of the teachers we have coached are among our closest friends now. Care about your coach because your coach absolutely cares about you.

## TEACHER SPOTLIGHT: RONELLE SWART

Ronelle Swart has been teaching history for over 20 years in South Africa.

*Why foster learning from peers?*

As a South African, I took inspiration about education from Nelson Mandela, our former president and world-renowned icon, when he said, "Education is the most powerful weapon which you can use to change the world." I always remember that when I stand in front of my students. It makes me realise what a huge privilege it is to be a teacher. As I grow older (I am almost 60 years old), I realise how little I know. This mindset of realising our own limitations is essential for learning from peers and other professionals.

*(Continued)*

As equals, teachers could learn a lot from each other. In a country like South Africa with its devastating former policy of racial segregation during the apartheid years from 1948–1994, this factor becomes even more important. The mindset of regarding all peers as equals regardless of race, gender, age, etc. is such a valuable asset to learn from peers. We should remember that each teacher in his/her unique way has a contribution to make and that we can learn from each other.

The moment teachers realise that there are other people experiencing the same problems and challenges in their careers, that might lessen their own burden. To be able to share experiences and to discuss events with others in the same profession is essential for a teacher's growth. On the positive side, it also helps to hear of other teachers' achievements and accomplishments. All of this could help teachers gather their strength and carry on with their jobs with renewed energy and motivation. The learning process is never finished, even for teachers who are highly qualified and very experienced. The Japanese proverb "To teach is to learn" applies here.

## ADMINISTRATOR SPOTLIGHT: TASHI WIDMER

Tashi Widmer is Executive Director at Caribbean Christian Centre for the Deaf in Jamaica.

*How do you foster learning from peers?*

Seek to understand before being understood. Ask questions for elaboration in order to best understand their thought processes. Assume the best in others. Affirm their sentiments and positive actions before offering constructive feedback for growth. It is possible for everyone to waver at least once, and I ought to be willing to forgive faults and give the benefit of the doubt before making a final conclusion about them.

In my efforts to best work with one culture wherein tension is constantly sensed, I was challenged by the idea that the most effective way to earn the trust of the staff members within that tense culture is to spend time with them as people, not as professionals to merely meet with and then leave. Just be present, listen, spend time getting to know them, and cherish them for who they are, regardless of their differences. After all, transparent and affirmative communication and positive rapport are the heart of healthy relationships. I attempt to listen more and ask more questions than offer solutions.

*Why foster learning from peers?*

There is a saying that it takes a village to raise a child. Likewise, it takes a community to have heightened knowledge and a vibrant learning circle. Everyone is "one of a kind" and therefore has different perspectives and insights to offer. From a circle of diverse beings, one can learn so much, whether this means reconditioning, conditioning, or un-conditioning something. "Relearning, learning, or unlearning" is a part of life. A community of learning helps to strengthen appreciation for diversity, a sense of ownership of the vision, teamwork, and dynamic knowledge, which should result in improved collaboration, job satisfaction, and recognition of varying abilities.

# RESOURCES

| LEARNING FROM PEERS KEY IDEAS | |
|---|---|
| **Workshops That Work: Renovating the One-Size-Fits-All Model** | Try implementing inquiry into workshops. Consider using the Evolving Learner Cycle of Inquiry: *focus, learn, refine, reflect.* |
| **Professional Learning Communities (PLCs)** | Look to reformat PLCs by including mindfulness; the Evolving Learner Cycle of Inquiry; and understanding Tuckman's model on the developmental stages of a team: forming, storming, norming, performing, adjourning. |
| **Coaching Principles and Practices** | Instructional coaching can be a powerful tool in learning from peers. Don't let not having a full-time coach get in the way. There are innovative approaches to utilize coaching. |
| **Feeling Connected, Seen, and Heard** | How are you connected, seen, and heard?<br><br>• Book clubs<br>• Take breaks<br>• #schoolhashtags<br>• Podcasts<br>• Restorative practices |
| **Renovating Professional Learning** | What are some ways to renovate professional learning now?<br><br>• Network meetings<br>• Master classes<br>• Day of innovation<br>• JOT (Just One Thing) |

## LEARNING FROM PEERS KEY IDEAS

| | |
|---|---|
| **Social-Emotional Learning** | Social-emotional learning (SEL) is the foundation and lens through which kid and adult learning is designed. Build your capacity by using<br><br>• Mindfulness activities<br>• Zones of Regulation<br>• Brain breaks<br>• Empathy<br>• Affirmations<br>• Social Thinking™<br>• Calm calendars<br>• Play |
| **Parents as Peers** | Involving parents/families as partners in our cycle of inquiry, we can design a solution that meets the needs of learners and removes a point of friction between home and school. |

# LEARN MORE FROM THOUGHT LEADERS WHO INSPIRE US TO LEARN FROM PEERS

**Read:**

Aguilar, E. (2013). *The art of coaching: Effective strategies for school transformation.* San Francisco, CA: Wiley.

Aguilar, E. (2016). *The art of coaching teams: Building resilient communities that transform schools.* San Francisco, CA: Jossey-Bass.

Bloomberg, P., & Pitchford, B. (2017). *Leading impact teams: Building a culture of efficacy.* Thousand Oaks, CA: Corwin.

Brown, B. (2018). *Dare to lead: Brave work. Tough conversations. Whole hearts.* London, UK: Ebury.

Dana, N. F., Thomas, C. H., & Boynton, S. (2011). *Inquiry: A districtwide approach to staff and student learning.* Thousand Oaks, CA: Corwin, a Joint Publication With Learning Forward.

Hammond, Z. (2015). *Culturally responsive teaching and the brain: Promoting authentic engagement and rigor among culturally and linguistically diverse students.* Thousand Oaks, CA: Corwin.

Immordino-Yang, M. H. (2016). *Emotions, learning, and the brain: Exploring the educational implications of affective neuroscience.* New York, NY: W. W. Norton.

Knight, J. (2016). *Better conversations: Coaching ourselves and each other to be more credible, caring, and connected.* Thousand Oaks, CA: Corwin.

Knight, J. (2018). *The impact cycle: What instructional coaches should do to foster powerful improvements in teaching.* Thousand Oaks, CA: Corwin.

Le Fevre, D., Timperley, H., Twyford, K., & Ell, F. (2020). *Leading powerful professional learning: Responding to complexity with adaptive expertise.* Thousand Oaks, CA: Corwin.

MacDonald, E. (2013). *The skillful team leader: A resource for overcoming hurdles to professional learning for student achievement.* Thousand Oaks, CA: Corwin Press, a Joint Publication With Learning Forward.

Mraz, K., Porcelli, A., & Tyler, C. (2016). *Purposeful play: A teacher's guide to igniting deep and joyful learning across the day.* Portsmouth, NH: Heinemann.

# LEARN MORE FROM THOUGHT LEADERS WHO INSPIRE US TO LEARN FROM PEERS

Schechter, C. (2020). *The wisdom of practice: Leading learning from success.* Thousand Oaks, CA: Corwin.

Siegel, D. J. (2010). *Mindsight: The new science of personal transformation.* New York, NY: Bantam Books.

Siegel, D. J., & Bryson, T. P. (2012). *The whole-brain child: 12 revolutionary strategies to nurture your child's developing mind.* New York, NY: Bantam Books.

Sweeney, D. (2011). *Student-centered coaching: A guide for K–8 coaches and principals.* Thousand Oaks, CA: Corwin.

## Watch:

Brené Brown: Brené Brown on Empathy (2013). The RSA (https://www.youtube.com/watch?v=1Evwgu369Jw)

Della Flora: Creative Ways to Get Kids to Thrive in School (2019). Ted Talk (ted.com/talks/olympia_della_flora_creative_ways_to_get_kids_to_thrive_in_school)

Bill Gates: Teachers Need Real Feedback (2013). Ted Talk (ted.com/talks/bill_gates_teachers_need_real_feedback)

Sir Ken Robinson: How to Escape Education's Death Valley (2013). Ted Talk (ted.com/talks/ken_robinson_how_to_escape_education_s_death_valley)

Linda Cliatt Wayman: How to Fix a Broken School? Lead Fearless, Love Hard (2015). Ted Talk (ted.com/talks/linda_cliatt_wayman_how_to_fix_a_broken_school_lead_fearlessly_love_hard)

## Listen:

Steve Barkley Ponders Out Loud podcast: barkleypd.com/blog/podcast-the-power-of-peers-students-supporting-students/

Educators Lead podcast: educatorslead.com/podcast/

Instructional Coaching Corner podcast: podcasts.apple.com/us/podcast/instructional-coaching-corner/id1155335310

Student-Centered Coaching podcast: dianesweeney.com/our-videos-podcasts/

*(Continued)*

(Continued)

## LEARN MORE FROM THOUGHT LEADERS WHO INSPIRE US TO LEARN FROM PEERS

**Explore:**

Elena Aguilar Bright Morning Team: brightmorningteam.com/

Instructional Coaching Group: instructionalcoaching.com/

Visit evolvinglearning.org for more.

## THOUGHTS, JOTS, AND NEXT STEPS

# CHAPTER 3

. . . . . . . . . .

# LEARNING FROM THE WORLD

is about
**honoring the learner**

through authentic, real-world connections

### THE WORLD

offers unlimited possibilities to

**BECOME AN EDU-EXPLORER**
to discover and share your
learning with kids and peers

**DEVELOP YOUR TRIBE**
by connecting to individuals
who have similar goals and ideas

**LEVERAGE SOCIAL MEDIA**
as a tool for sharing, answer-seeking,
connecting, and idea-generating

To be effective we must

**FILTER**   **EDIT**   **FOCUS**   **BALANCE**

# HONOR THE LEARNER: WORLD

> "A man's real education begins after he has left school. True education is gained through the discipline of life."
>
> —Henry Ford

Think back to when you were a young student. Where were you sitting? Who did the talking? As we have discussed before, we likely all were taught in similar ways, with forward-facing desks and teachers who released all the information. But has that changed as we have entered the education profession? We have all sat in classrooms where an instructor stood at the front and released information when and how that teacher believed was appropriate. Experience and research make it clear that engagement is key to learning, and innovative teachers and leaders are focusing on learning experiences that are collaborative, inquiry-based, and learner-driven. However, while the model of teaching kids is changing, there appears to be very little innovation in professional learning for educators. Nothing burns like the sting of irony when you are sitting in a professional development session about the benefits of flexible seating while sitting in rows of forward-facing desks or listening to a direct-instruction lecture about how to teach in a more collaborative, creative manner.

NOTHING BURNS LIKE THE STING OF IRONY WHEN YOU ARE SITTING IN A PROFESSIONAL DEVELOPMENT SESSION ABOUT THE BENEFITS OF FLEXIBLE SEATING WHILE SITTING IN ROWS OF FORWARD-FACING DESKS OR LISTENING TO A DIRECT-INSTRUCTION LECTURE ABOUT HOW TO TEACH IN A MORE COLLABORATIVE, CREATIVE MANNER.

Consider the "Who is working hardest in the classroom?" visual we shared in Chapter 1. It is so frustrating and perplexing to see that teachers still experience professional development in a "sit and get," one-size-fits-all, top-down, antiquated model that directly opposes the learning models that we want for our kids. Professional development, in fact, is generally something that happens *to* teachers, rather than something that educators independently pursue based on their interest, the ever-changing tide of education, or the needs of their learners.

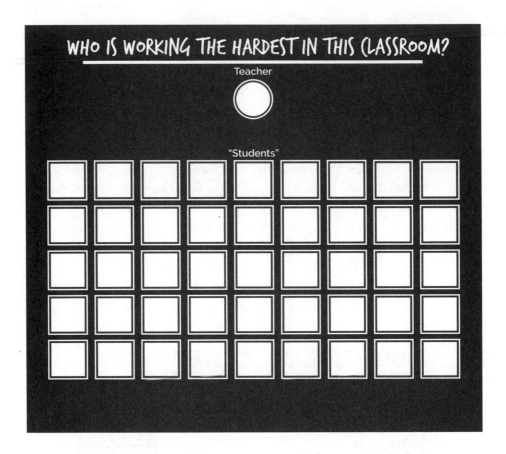

Rather than getting into all the reasons that educators are taught in this manner (Who has that kind of time?), we will focus on actionable solutions. Teachers are nothing if not innovative, and in taking the reins of our own professional learning, driven by intention, moral imperatives, and interests at the forefront, we can and *must* channel our energies into opportunities for ourselves and our teams.

## Unlimited Possibilities

The ability to learn from anyone around the world, people we may never even see face-to-face, is truly astounding. If we think back just 15 or 20 years ago, our options for learning beyond our site were so limited and largely consisted of conferences. The explosion of the web and the unlimited possibilities for learning we now have as educators, in many ways, molded teachers into a new kind of "pro-

*Source:* Courtesy of pixabay.com

fessional learning explorer"—those who seek to improve themselves and their careers with purpose and intent.

Technology has changed the world in incredible ways, and that, in turn, must transform education and learning. Educators and educational leaders are helping to develop the future workforce and individuals who will help run, fix, operate, and build the world of tomorrow in roles that have yet to even be invented. However, the educational system and the way that teachers improve their practice have changed very little. As discussed in the introduction, we do not need to *wait* for a complete systemic change in order to significantly alter the way we run schools and classrooms. We all have the opportunity to be constantly learning from the world around us.

*Source:* unsplashed.com/@dariuszsankowski

## BECOMING AN EDU-EXPLORER

In the digital age, it is easier than ever to explore. Spend 15 minutes on your smartphone, and you may start with a recipe, follow some links, and end up watching a video about mid-century modern furniture. Opportunities for exploration are all around us, all the time. However, finding something impactful and transferring it into targeted change or innovative ideas can be a larger challenge. In ages past, explorers were leaders, boldly going forth to discover the unknown. However, the job didn't stop there. Explorers were charged with not only going forth and finding something new, but also *bringing it back* for the good of the community. Teachers and educational leaders can learn from this. Yes, you can look at a Pinterest board, read an educational article, join a Facebook group of professionals, or follow an educational leader's blog. You may even take what you learn and implement it in your classroom. However, it is in the sharing of knowledge and ideas that we carry that learning to the next level. This sharing helps to cultivate long-term growth.

As an *edu-explorer*, you are charged with charting unknown waters not only for the good of your own learners, but for the community at large. When you find something new, share it. That is what propels professional learning for us all.

## DEVELOPING YOUR TRIBE

> "Find your tribe. Let yourself be seen. You are already someone's hero."
>
> —Vironika Tugaleva

As we discussed in the previous chapters, "Learning From Kids" and "Learning From Peers," feeling seen and valued is a key need to ensure engagement and personal satisfaction in learning. Beyond feeling valued, however, it is essential for those in education to develop a tribe of individuals who will help you grow, develop, persevere, and improve. You need the mentor who will give you honest and encouraging feedback, the colleague who inspires you to step out of your comfort zone, the teacher who comes up with insanely great ideas, and the educator who stretches your thinking and helps inspire your next steps. This is your tribe. Your tribe is not merely there to make you feel safe in your career and good about yourself. In fact, you may not even know some of your tribe outside of the digital realm. Your tribe is naturally comprised of people who are physically close to you in proximity—your grade-level/department team, your leadership, and of course your learners—but the tribe doesn't have to end there. There may be individuals who are outside of your school—even on the other side of the globe—who inspire, challenge, and support you and your professional goals.

*Source:* unsplashed.com/@timmarshall

If you are *exceptionally* lucky, you will connect instantly with your team on a personal and professional level where you can easily share ideas, lesson plan together, provide honest feedback, and inspire each other daily. They will send you great articles on the weekend (and read the ones you send them), give you an honest opinion on your recent idea to completely overhaul your classroom management, give you the supportive boosts you desperately need on bad days, encourage you to try that new grading system (and help you set it up), and know just when to bring you a much-needed coffee. However, it is more than likely that at some point in your career, you will be the explorer of your tribe, and you will be the one venturing out into the world to bring back the best ideas and the inspiration for your team. We all need to connect to individuals who have similar goals and ideas, or ones that positively help us look in new directions. We also all need people in our lives who will push us, encourage us, question us, help us, and inspire us. It helps us all get through rough times; improves learner performance; lowers rates of teacher burnout; and, frankly, makes the profession more rewarding. We know that we can learn from our *kids* and our *peers*, but what about what the rest of *the world* has to offer?

## SOCIAL MEDIA

One way to develop your tribe and connect with people is on social media. At the time of this writing, the most popular tools are Twitter, Instagram, and Facebook, but much more important than the specific tools are the relationships and the learning that the tools enable. Social media can be used for many functions, including sharing, answer-seeking, connecting, and idea-generating. However, many of us on social media platforms typically linger in one of these categories casually and never thoughtfully combine them. It is in the strategic *combination* of these areas that the power of social media for professional growth truly starts to emerge.

> "The best way to get started on the path to sharing your work is to think about what you want to learn, and make a commitment to learning it in front of others."
> —Austin Kleon

As educators and learners, we can use social media in a cycle of inquiry to improve our practice. For example, once a problem of practice has been identified, we can search social media (e.g., Twitter, Instagram) for inspiration, ideas, and solutions using a specific hashtag. (If you aren't sure what hashtags to start with, try a basic search like "#secondgrademath," "#informationliteracy," or "#lifescience." Notice the hashtags being used in the results you are most interested in, and try searching those specific hashtags as well. You may stumble upon a hashtag used by experts in the field that offers a great opportunity to make a real-world connection.) Once you find an idea/solution that matches your problem of practice, develop a plan to implement the strategy. Evaluate the impact of the strategy on teaching and learning, and iterate as necessary. Be sure to share your challenges and successes with your colleagues face-to-face and via social media. We are all learning together! Note: This cycle of inquiry also works for learners in our classroom, and teachers are the guides regarding what is age appropriate.

## The Fear of the Unknown

If you work in education or have children of your own, you may feel skepticism, fear, or even hatred of social media. News articles emerge every day describing how social media use leads to bullying, violence, and even suicide. There is no doubt that social media for children and teens is a tool that can veer wildly out of control without constant monitoring by informed and interested adults, ongoing lessons in digital citizenship, and strict usage guidelines. The exhausting efforts required of adults surrounding the usage of social media might even lead people to question whether it is a useful tool or a dangerous nuisance that should be banned. In our experience, many educators and parents avoid social media altogether, believing that it is either too much trouble to bother with, meant for "young people," or a hated annoyance with which they would rather not engage. If you are an adult who has felt this way or avoided social media for another reason, we encourage you to hear us out and take another look. Social media, when used thoughtfully and well, could be the most powerful source of professional learning that you have ever found.

Looking at our Evolving Learner Cycle of Inquiry, social media can be consumed and utilized in a thoughtful way to grow and improve in your practice. The cycle of *focus–learn–refine–reflect* will be described throughout this section. The first step in approaching social media for the purpose of professional learning is to *focus* on what you need or would like to learn. However, even when you focus on and engage in a desired topic, you need to narrow your search. From there, you will move into connecting and communicating to *learn* from others. After sourcing information, topics, and connections, you will *refine* what you will actually take in and bring back to your school or classroom. Finally, this ongoing cycle will always move through with *reflection*: What did you learn? Whom did you meet? Was it worth your time? Where will you go next? Did what you implemented have a positive impact? Once again, the cycle is not always in perfect order, but utilizing the steps will help you to approach social media with intention that will help you learn, grow, and connect with the world of education and professional learning.

## Personal Promotion vs. Sharing Your Story

"Tell the story of the mountain you climbed. Your words could become a page in someone else's survival guide."
—Morgan Harper Nichols

We've all seen it on various social media platforms: *I'm engaged! We bought a house! I got my dream job! We're pregnant! I had pizza for dinner!* Highly curated self-promotion is the very bread and butter of social media. However, it is nowhere near the best of what social media has to offer. As a learner, it is critical to understand how powerful sharing your work—not just personal promotion—can be on a professional level. When first accessing social media for professional growth, it is easy to follow others, read, learn, and grow. However, opening up and sharing in this space can often be very intimidating and requires vulnerability. Working in education, we all invest pieces of ourselves into what we do, so it is natural to fear criticism or even less-than-glowing feedback. We encourage you to put those fears to the side in favor of adding to the growth and inspiration of others. Sharing your story is the best way to invite the world into your classroom or school and spotlight the amazing things that are happening for your learners. The learning that happens on social media should be about give and take. When you share your best, others can learn from you and vice versa.

Kendall is a principal at a mid-sized elementary school. Kendall's staff were a hardworking and creative team of educators who were regularly producing engaging and impactful projects and experiences for their learners. The school had also recently developed a makerspace and innovation space funded by grants, filled with some of the latest technology and exciting new tools that engaged learners and inspired deeper learning. Kendall provided professional learning regularly on the technology, and teachers were loving the opportunity to push the envelope with their instruction. In fact, several teachers and principals from other schools even visited the school to learn how to improve. So imagine Kendall's surprise when she pushed out a parent/family survey about school progress and received low marks on *The school utilizes technology regularly* and *My student is learning with new technology*! By all accounts, her school was not only excelling in these areas but leading the pack! So why did the parents and the community see something different? Because they had no idea what was happening at the school. Kendall's school did not promote the amazing gains the school had made with the makerspace and professional learning to their families through social media or other means. They were not telling their story! In the absence of evidence or facts, many onlookers will often write their *own* story for a school. This could be as innocuous as, "My sister's friend's son went to that school, and they do NO ART!" to a slightly more alarming, "I heard that school doesn't teach reading OR math because they don't think students deserve it!" Regardless of how ridiculous a story may sound, we live in an age of trusting personal recommendations. This very premise is what makes many bloggers, YouTubers, and social media "influencers" so popular and successful! Ignoring the fact that many people develop narratives in the absence of fact is a dangerous game. Don't allow outsiders to promote disinformation, misunderstandings, or half-truths about your sacred learning community where you pour in blood, sweat, tears, and hours; share, share, share!

On a more macro level, schools and districts can also benefit greatly from social media. The utilization of a social media account can serve as a communication tool for families and students, and it can also open up the schools to the community and the outside world, again promoting all the great things that are happening on the inside. Beyond this, schools and districts continually drive professional learning and growth through sharing and generating ideas and conversation around their successes. Such conversations help develop networks of learners who can help and share with each other.

We often say that if you don't open your doors and tell the story of what is happening in your classroom or school, others will make up the story for you. Therefore, inviting the world into your space—whether it is a classroom, school, or even district—can not only demonstrate the things that you and your team are doing, but it can also help others understand the perspective of the teachers and students inside. By inviting virtual visitors into schools, we all show the changing tide of education and reveal differences and similarities that may reach a global scale.

Of course, the idea of sharing can also bring up many other emotions for educators and leaders, including anxiety, insecurity, doubt, and worry: *Why should I show anything when I'm not an expert on it? No one wants to see what I'm doing anyway. What if people hate what I share?* These doubts and feelings are normal, but truly unfounded. As educators and leaders, we are part of a supportive, thriving community of people who truly want to learn from one another. Assume positive intent! After all, we spend our days encouraging kids to collaborate and share with one another. We also put a huge effort into helping students improve their self-confidence and believe in themselves, but many times that does not carry over into our own lives. Believe us: There is something that you are doing in your class/school/district right now that someone else wants to learn or know about. In fact, there are likely *lots* of things you are doing that people want to learn about. Unless you quit your job right now and do a traveling road show, the best way to share those things is on social media.

## Answer-Seeking

> "The most valuable resource that all teachers have is each other. Without collaboration, our growth is limited to our own perspectives."
>
> —Robert John Meehan

Let's go back in time to the age of BT (before Twitter) or BYT (before YouTube). How did we learn *anything*? We shamelessly admit to asking Twitter friends and watching YouTube tutorials to learn about things from how to fix a leaky faucet to the best way to cook a chicken. Before this information age (though our memory seems foggy), we likely would have consulted a book. With teaching and learning, it wasn't much different: Want to learn the best way to teach math? Buy the book. Need more discipline ideas? Read this book. Confused on how to write lesson plans? You get the idea. As you may have surmised, we appreciate the value of books enough to have devoted the past few years to coauthoring the book you are currently reading! However, we know now that in many instances there are *many different ways* to approach a problem or situation and that answers are constantly changing. In addition, there will be moments when the people around you may not have the answer (or perhaps don't have the answer you want or need). In that instance, where do you go? Social media.

Jack is a second-grade teacher. Two years ago, Jack's district announced that there would be a significant shift in science instruction. This shift would move from his state's science standards to the new Next Generation Science Standards (NGSS). The NGSS was multilayered, nuanced, and an unbelievably extreme shift from previous instruction. In addition, the NGSS was presented with little professional learning alongside it and with few ideas and curriculum to support teachers. To say that Jack felt lost and insecure in moving forward with the NGSS would be an understatement. As Jack reports, "I felt so confused, and literally no one else in my school—or even district—seemed to have a good enough grasp on it to help me out." So Jack became an explorer and turned to the community who had helped him out in numerous other situations: Twitter. "As soon as I searched for #NGSS, I saw that there were teachers in my grade level across the country who had experience, tips, and were willing to help—it was huge," Jack states. "Suddenly, my desperation melted away and I felt empowered." Not only that, but Jack was then eager to share what he learned with colleagues. This sharing helped to empower and improve the attitudes of the teachers around him. The willing help of an open community of people who have experience in any area where we need answers, whether it be teaching science or cooking a chicken, can transform a frustrating and lonely situation into a moment of growth and empowerment.

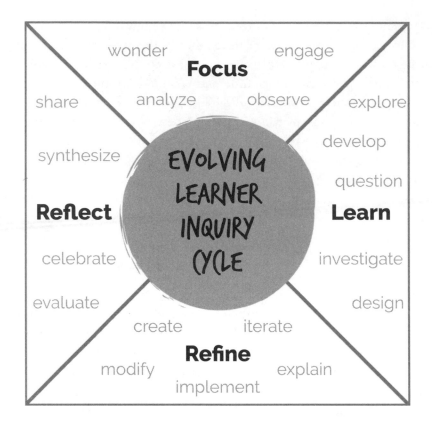

## Professional Learning

> "Collaboration allows teachers to capture each other's fund of collective intelligence."
>
> —Mike Schmoker

Sometimes, instead of seeking answers to specific or finite questions, we seek to learn something completely new. Having the mindset of "I don't know what I don't know" is critical to an evolving learner! Imagine this familiar struggle: You stumble upon and read an article about a math approach called Cognitively Guided Instruction. You would love to learn more about the approach and even be connected to resources and support on the topic. However, your district is focusing its time (and money) on training teachers in language arts instruction and not math. What do you do?

Many teachers might feel apathetic, frustrated, and annoyed that they do not have choice in their professional learning. We've all been there. However, the idea of having no choice is actually a myth. Social media provides unlimited options for learning on virtually every topic. A quick tour on Twitter will reveal teachers and communities across the country who are utilizing Cognitively Guided Instruction and are excited to share resources and ideas, as well as provide tips and answer questions. The only thing it costs is time, and it is our experience that time invested in professional learning via social media often pays off when you discover an innovative lesson that someone else has already designed or when you find a protocol that allows you and your team to recapture time. Ever heard of a stand-up meeting? By following a hashtag like #StandUpMeeting, in a few minutes you can learn about an innovative new way to conduct a team or staff meeting that can completely change the dynamic and culture of your organization. Again, just with a few minutes, a hashtag, and an open mind, you can improve your practice and share your learning with your peers.

## Connecting

"Communication—the human connection—is the key to personal and career success."

—Paul J. Meyer

Let's face it, teaching can be a lonely, isolated profession. This may seem counterintuitive, given that you spend all day surrounded by humans with whom you are interacting constantly. However, all educators and leaders need different professional relationships and friendships, outside of teacher–kid or boss–employee interactions. Individuals who can answer questions, allow us to vent, and help us generate new ideas are essential. These are the people we need to be learning with, so we want to include them in our tribe. The good news is, these relationships can absolutely be found on social media, if you know what you are looking for. Whether in online chats, reading someone's posts, or simply scrolling through someone's page or blog, you will find like-minded people who will bring out multiple professional facets you may have not even considered before. Equally important, we should also aim to find those who have different perspectives, interests, and opinions from our own. There is much to be gained through different kinds of connections. The key is to never pigeonhole your expectations. When you open your eyes to possibilities, your gains will expand immensely. Next time you are searching social media, see if you find people who belong in your tribe.

### Social Media Archetypes

*Source:* iStockphoto.com/portfolio/pop_jop

Archetypes are a typical example of behavior or personality and can be found all around us. You may remember high school essays about literary archetypes (*The Everyman! The Hero! The Villain!*), but archetypes can also be applied to the world of social media. Certainly, every person you encounter, whether face-to-face or online, is different and an individual, but often characteristic roles and personalities will stand out and fall into common categories. This can be especially true when utilizing social media for the purpose of sourcing ideas and professional learning material. While we don't aim to "label" individuals, archetypes can be an especially useful filtering tool in the vastness of social media to help you organize and navigate. After a *lot* of time spent online and in the realm of education through social media, we have developed what we feel are common social media archetypes that you will likely encounter. It is important to note that there is no "best" or "worst" in this list, and it is by no means exhaustive. However, there is something to gain or learn from each of these archetypes.

### The Mentor

You know immediately when you find this person. The mentor is experienced and able to talk through those experiences. You can trust the person's judgment and direction because the individual has *been there*. You can one day envision yourself being in that person's shoes. Though you may never speak to the Mentor face-to-face, you can admire this person from afar and still learn something.

## The Mirror

The Mirror is a like-minded colleague who can offer advice without reservation because this person knows what you are aspiring toward or looking for. Maybe the Mirror teaches the same grade level or content area. This person knows your struggles and when you ask a question, you know you will get an honest answer. The Mirror on a social media platform is beautiful when you can find it. Mirrors are not caught up in your personal relationship or other details of your life, because they are not a part of it. They are focused on helping you with a particular professional need and can even ask you tough questions. The Mirror understands your direction and can help you get there.

## The Challenger

Ah, the Challenger. You may encounter this person and immediately want to cast this person aside. You ask a question about inclusion during an online chat, and the Challenger is ready for battle: *"How can we provide a quality education for all students when inclusion spreads resources thin?"* You might immediately take offense, get irritated or angry, or brush the person off. However, there are takeaways from the Challenger. Do Challengers immediately agree with you? No. Do they present questions that make you think about things you hadn't considered? Maybe! Do not make the mistake of thinking of the Challenger as a careless critic; this person's point of view can broaden your perspective on how your decisions may ultimately be viewed by others.

## The Rockstar

The Rockstar has scores of followers, an immaculate classroom, stellar lessons, a cute wardrobe, and you are fairly sure this person is sponsored by Elmer's glue or Astrobrights paper. Amid the chaos of daily work life, the Rockstar manages to maintain an impressive social media presence, daily YouTube posts, and an adorable blog that brings tears to your eyes. You can't help but be drawn to the Rockstar and this person's perfect existence. You know you will never be the Rockstar, *and that's okay.* For now, it's fun to be in the crowd, note a few fun ideas, and marvel at the Rockstar's ability to "do it all." Just don't get caught up in the highly curated hype, and know we all have real lives—you are never meant to aspire to perfection.

## The Compass

Your Compass can be found nearly anywhere. Maybe you chatted with the person a few times. Perhaps this person was your Mirror (or Challenger), but you've continued to follow each other's path and forged a friendship. You have similar goals and values, admire each other, and have found a connection that may span states or continents. You can trust your Compass to answer your frantic emails about lessons or staff meetings, and you listen to each other's rants and worries. This connection is what makes social media such an amazing platform in a professional space. There are honest, hardworking, good individuals who are looking to connect with others like them to help improve the profession, learning, and lives, all for the sake of our kids.

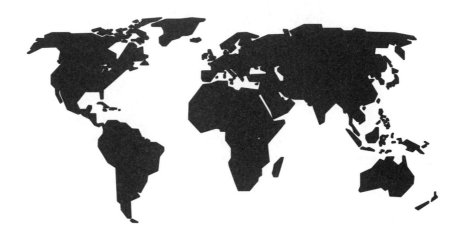

### *Creating Your Ideal Learning Environment*

Finding inspiration and ideas on existing platforms such as social media, websites, or blogs can be a springboard toward amazing connection and ideas. However, even the smallest idea can be catapulted into a completely new venture for connection. To help explain, let's hear from Andrew Stadel, a math teacher and the brains behind Estimation 180 at estimation180.com.

I began my teaching career and number sense journey in 2003. As a middle school math teacher, my students would frequently ask, "Mr. Stadel, how tall are you?"

Since I tower over most middle school students, it's only natural for students to be curious about my height, especially that first week of school when they meet me for the first time. It was about an 8-year journey to realize students have this natural intuition of magnitude—the ability to compare one number to another number. During those 8 years, I was not only ignorant of my students' intuitive sense of magnitude, but was also failing to engage students in rich and meaningful mathematical conversations. Specifically, I failed when I revealed my height to students immediately after being asked, "How tall are you?"

It wasn't until about 2011 when my number sense journey took a different direction. I began delaying the reveal of my height and would respond with, "How tall do you think I am?" My intention was not to deflect. My intention was to now engage students in a mental exercise where they would strategically choose a height for Mr. Stadel that made sense to them. By engaging in this exercise, I placed a greater emphasis on the mathematical thinking students are capable of doing on a daily basis. To illustrate this point, consider the difference between the following two conversations:

Conversation 1 (typical 2003–2011):

| | |
|---|---|
| **Student:** | Mr. Stadel, how tall are you? |
| **Mr. Stadel:** | Six foot four inches. |
| **Student:** | Wow. That's tall. My dad is six foot two [inches]. |

Conversation 2 (typical 2011–present):

| | |
|---|---|
| **Student:** | Mr. Stadel, how tall are you? |
| **Mr. Stadel:** | How tall do you think I am? |
| **Student:** | Can I stand next to you? |
| **Mr. Stadel:** | Yes. [Student stands next to me.] |
| **Mr. Stadel:** | Tell me what you're thinking about or figuring out by standing next to me. |
| **Student:** | My dad is six foot two [inches], and you seem a little taller than him. |
| **Mr. Stadel:** | It sounds like you're saying I can't be shorter than six foot two inches. What's a height that's too tall for me? |
| **Student:** | Ten feet. |

(Continued)

**Mr. Stadel:**    You're right. I don't know anyone that is ten feet tall. That's the height of a bas-ketball rim! Now that you've had a chance to stand next to me, about how tall do you think I am?

**Student:**    I'd say six foot five inches.

**Mr. Stadel:**    I'm six foot . . . [pause for dramatic effect] four inches.

**Student:**    Oh, dang. I was so close. I was off by one inch.

**Mr. Stadel:**    You should be proud of your six foot five. I asked, "How tall do you think I am?" and you found a strategy that made sense to you by standing next to me, and you used your dad's height as a comparison.

Conversation 1 is obviously shorter. However, let's not lose sight of how it ignored the student's intuition and sense of magnitude. I would frequently hear students mention some reference after I had revealed my height. They already had some other height to compare my height to, and this indicated a sense of magnitude. Intuitively, they were ready and willing to use what they knew about their dad's height.

Conversation 2 honors the student's intuition and sense of magnitude. When asking students to estimate my height, I started noticing students intuitively had a stronger desire to design a strategy and engage in a mental exercise using references meaningful to them (in this case, their dad's height). Once I started tuning into these conversations with students in 2011, my number sense journey became more meaningful and interesting. Little did I know, my number sense journey was about to get hijacked.

In January 2012, I received an email from my good friend Brian Kays, and the email subject line simply read, "Thought you would enjoy this video." The video link took me to Dan Meyer's TEDx Talk, "Math Class Needs a Makeover" (ted.com/talks/dan_meyer_math_curriculum_makeover). My lens for teaching and learning math was greatly transformed after watching Meyer's talk. I immediately tracked down Meyer's blog where I found numerous math lessons, ideas, and classroom reflections from his experiences as a high school math teacher. One fea-ture Meyer frequently included in his lessons was estimation challenges. I was inspired by Meyer's work and began incorporating estimation challenges into my lessons. I would type up questions on a presentation slide and include it with daily math warm-ups. I thought these questions were fun, but quickly discovered the questions fell flat with students. For example, a question like "How many black keys are on a piano?" would immediately result in student responses like "I have no idea." Upon reflecting on this process, I realized the students lacked both a connection to these abstract estimation challenges and a point of reference that would allow them to better strategize a reasonable estimate. I put these types of estimation challenges on hold. I knew there was potential, but I needed time to reevaluate the format and purpose of estimation challenges.

During that summer, I read a book by Steve Leinwand titled *Accessible Mathematics: Ten Instructional Shifts That Raise Student Achievement*. One of Leinwand's instructional shifts is Building Number Sense, and he lists estimation as a key ingredient. Leinwand's book helped me realize that whenever students asked about my height, they were able to better engage in an estimation challenge because the format provided both a personal connection and point of reference to use for their strategy. Therefore, I made it a goal for the 2012–2013 school year to include estimation challenges in a format that provided visual references and built on prior knowledge from previous days. Since there are traditionally 180 days in a school year, I set out to provide my students with 180 estimation challenges, where Day 1 is "How tall is Mr. Stadel?" The second estimation challenge (Day 2) is a picture of Mr. and Mrs. Stadel, and students are asked, "What is the height of Mrs. Stadel?" The visual provides students with a point of reference and prior knowledge in order to make a strategic estimate of Mrs. Stadel's height.

By a couple weeks into the 2012–2013 school year, I was quickly accumulating estimation challenges. My students were able to engage in conversations by sharing their mathematical thinking and strategies. I realized these estimation challenges shouldn't stay trapped in my classroom and decided to share with other math teachers interested in using them with their students. On September 28, 2012, teachers everywhere could engage in these estimation challenges to help strengthen student number sense at Estimation 180 (estimation180.com). Estimation 180 now holds over 200 visual estimation challenges where students are asked a quantifiable question based on the visual provided. Students and teachers are encouraged to have a conversation around reasonable ranges, magnitude, and strategies before revealing the answer. Estimation 180 contains numerous series of estimation challenges that include concepts such as capacity, height, time, and other quantities while using objects that range from food to toilet paper.

Since 2012, my number sense journey has been enriched when teachers and students share how Estimation 180 is their favorite part of math class or that students have created their own estimation challenges. I'm honored and humbled that Estimation 180 has provided opportunities for both teachers and students to engage in mathematical conversations and build number sense one day at a time.

In many ways, Andrew Stadel's story is unique, but we can also pull out a lot of familiar scenarios from within it. Andrew was constantly evaluating what happened in his classroom and was struggling with aspects of his teaching—as we all do—without a clear way to get help or guidance. Andrew was communicating regularly with his students *(learning from kids),* and a single email from a colleague sharing a video *(learning from peers)* led him to seek out answers from a blog and then social media *(learning from the world).* In learning more and refining his practice, he elected to share with others and build a professional learning community with his development of Estimation 180. Andrew followed the Evolving Learner Cycle of Inquiry of *focus–learn–refine–reflect* on this journey as well. Sometimes as educators, our best innovations and changes develop from hunches or small beliefs that we could improve something. However, where to start can be the most daunting task. Like Andrew, we can all look around at the wealth of resources at our fingertips, the kids in our classrooms, and our colleagues to drive us into learning and change.

## Idea-Generating

A common ailment has plagued authors and scribes for centuries: the dreaded writer's block. The idea that, well, you are *out of ideas.* It brings work to a grinding halt, saps hope and motivation in a single blow, and makes time crawl. As terrible as this sounds, we educators know there is a far worse affliction: teacher's block. *Teacher's block* occurs when you are fresh out of ways to innovate curriculum, bereft of ways to present new methods of learning, and devoid of ways to excite or motivate students—or worse, yourself. This ailment makes the school day drag; your interactions with students, parents, and coworkers painful, boring, or awkward; and can even be known to make you doubt yourself and your abilities. But have hope, colleagues: There is a cure! Through answer-seeking, connecting, and idea-generating on social media, you can get your creative juices flowing and start invigorating your practice with fresh and innovative ideas!

> "Teamwork divides the tasks and multiplies the successes."
> —Author Unknown

Ideas are the antidote to teacher's block. Generating all good ideas is not only unrealistic, but impossible. Teachers are shameless "thieves" of great ideas ("Oh, this bulletin board? I stole it from Tracey"), but sometimes it can be hard to know where to look to get the next great "take," thus paralyzing even the best educator or leader and keeping us clinging to what we already know. This can get anyone stuck in a rut, and create boredom or resentment toward work, and spur resignation and desperation.

What we know is that ideas breed invigoration and enhanced excitement about work, but the overflowing font of the internet can prove to be daunting in your hour of need. Where do you begin? First, look outside of your school. What is everyone doing? You can start small, such as by looking for something like classroom decor, or you could search for something more multifaceted, like how to develop a classroom management system that incorporates restorative justice, or how to teach a writer's workshop to struggling readers. Just remember this: If you want to find something, you will. In fact, more often than not, you won't know you are looking for something but manage to find that as well.

> "Getting information off the internet is like taking a drink from a fire hydrant."
>
> —Popularly attributed to Mitchell Kapor

## TIPS: FILTER, EDIT, FOCUS, BALANCE

How to begin when you are searching the internet for ideas? The blessing and curse of social media are in its abundance. The internet overflows with ideas, materials, people, and opinions. However, we all know that the World Wide Web is not solely populated with certified experts with all the right answers. In fact, it can be hard to see or distinguish the good, bad, and ugly when we are short on time, high in need, and frazzled—not to mention, even when we do have time, how do we eliminate confirmation bias, the tendency to seek out evidence as confirmation of what we believe or want to believe? How can we evaporate some of the social media ocean into a manageable professional learning pond?

## Filter

Setting some initial filters can save you loads of time when searching for good ideas. As noted in the Social Media section earlier in this chapter, a great initial filter is to search a hashtag. Simply put, a *hashtag* is a file folder of sorts, organizing a post into a category or titled group. Hashtags can be found on most major social media platforms, from Twitter and Instagram to Facebook and Pinterest. Rather than typing "math lesson ideas" into Google and sifting through 5 million hits you don't need, you would do better to search a hashtag on Twitter such as #secondgrademath, #iteachmath, or #MTBOS (Math Teacher Blog-o-Sphere—trust us, it's awesome). Education and leadership hashtags filled with ideas and rich content filter down to practitioners who utilize them. This is often more beneficial than relying on a search engine algorithm to search for key words. Those who are doing the work in the field and wanting to share will often be the predominant users of these hashtags. Notice we said *often*. Not everyone who uses a hashtag will be doing it to promote educational practices. Some—gasp!—may simply be looking for followers or click traffic. While annoying, the sifting is minimal compared to your average internet search.

While it is possible to find a hashtag on virtually any topic you may want to investigate, here are some awesome hashtags you may want to check out (across multiple platforms):

| General Interest | |
| --- | --- |
| #edchat | #educhat |
| #whyiteach | #edpolicy |
| #observeme | #schoolisreal |
| **Math** | |
| #MTBOS | #iteachmath |
| #elemmath | #alg1chat |
| #estimation180 | #3actmath |
| **English/Language Arts** | |
| #iteachreading | #RWYK |
| #kidlit | #CCchat |

| Science | |
|---|---|
| #STEAM/#STEM | #makerspace |
| #scichat | #NGSS |
| **Visual and Performing Arts** | |
| #artsed | #musedchat |
| #visualarts | #dramateacher |
| **Leadership and Coaching** | |
| #edleadership | #cpchat |
| #edadmin | #leadfromwithin |
| #edtechcoach | #observeme |
| **Instructional Practices** | |
| #PBL | #makered |
| #formativeassessment | #designthinking |
| #blendedlearning | #restorativejustice |
| **Inspiration and Motivation** | |
| #kidsdeservoit | #growthmindset |
| #SEL | #lifelonglearner |

## Edit

When on a specific search, the filtering of a hashtag will only take you so far before you get sucked into your screen, viewing content you do not need, or worse—cat videos! To avoid this pitfall, ask yourself these three simple questions: *Who am I? What do I need?* and *Why am I here?* For example, let's say you are a fourth-grade teacher searching for poetry to help with reading fluency. Suddenly, you find yourself sucked into a high school drama teacher's blog about her recent triumph with a production of *Death of Salesman*. While intriguing or even inspiring, this is not what you came for. *You teach fourth grade. You need poems. You have no business here.* The frequent personal reset to remind yourself of your purpose will save countless hours of aimless searches, and it will help you regain your focus. As we stated before, even if you aren't looking for something, you will still find it. Keep your center, edit your searches for what you need, and nag yourself about why you need it. You can also edit yourself by thinking about who you want the content to come from. Are you looking for content from a practitioner, an academic, an author, or a vendor? All four potentially have things to offer for poetry, but you might want to edit out all but the authors because you are hoping to connect your class with the actual poet.

## Focus

This section on focus could easily also be called, "Beware the Rabbit Hole." Much like the cat video pitfall of not editing your searches, the internet rabbit hole can take you from one turn to the next until you can't even retrace your steps or remember where you started. You start off wanting to find a writing lesson, and before you know it, you have spent 30 minutes scrolling through #neonclassroomdecor. How do you avoid something catching your eye and taking you away from your purpose?

First, know that it is fine to explore (and encouraged!), but stay in your lane. Remember your second-grade poetry search? Perhaps your initial searches bring you to articles about using plays in elementary school to help increase literacy. Is it exactly what you are looking for? No. But is it in your lane and directed toward what you need? Absolutely. However, each subsequent search runs the risk of taking you further from your goal if you don't keep your focus. Most of us would agree that not much can be directly gained by learning the methods of a high school drama teacher when you are focusing on primary reading fluency. Again, there is nothing wrong with exploring. However, when time is a precious resource and you know you need something specific, remember your purpose.

*Source:* unsplashed.com/@officialdavery

## Balance

Balance is something that many of us strive for, yet rarely achieve, in so many aspects of our lives. Balance with family, work, goals, desires—the list goes on and on. The desire to both "dive deep" and get what you need, without getting lost or sucking up all of your time, is a real concern. The internet, information, and social media are virtually limitless, so you are never really "done" when you are searching or learning. The key? Realizing that fact.

When we filter, edit, and focus what we are seeking, we also need to set limits on ourselves in both time and scope. While you may be seeking information on a math workshop, you simply will *never* consume all there is to know about that topic. Get what you need, and get out. It makes you a more purposeful consumer of information and helps you protect your time and, frankly, your sanity.

Speaking of sanity and balance, *don't* use social media to compare yourself to others. This is a real problem for adults and kids and not just in education. When we see an edited/curated version of someone else, it is easy to get a "comparison hangover." *Do* use social media to compare your current practice to previous practices you shared with your learning community so that you can concentrate on how you have grown as a professional.

## LURK NO MORE

We have focused a lot on how to get the most out of social media for your own benefit and, admittedly, a lot can be gained by simply searching blogs and boards, reading other people's chats, and sifting through those hashtags. But we encourage you no, *implore you*—to not be a perpetual *lurker* surfing the internet. The world of information available online is only as good as those feeding into it. Not only can you gain far more in chatting and interacting with others online (trust us—it's how we all met!), but believe it or not, you have *a lot* to share with others. Anxiety and doubt can creep in when we think of sharing out ideas, tips, or experiences. However, we guarantee that others are waiting to hear your experiences and can learn from them. Start small: Comment on posts, and ask questions in groups. Think about sharing one small thing a day. From there, you can move on to participating in live Twitter chats or even posting your own original content. Education has always been driven by the creativity and innovation of educators who look to innovate, create, and change things to improve learning for students. When we stop sharing, asking questions, or generating new ideas through conversation, we only serve to limit ourselves and others and shrink or eliminate growth and change. As educators and evolving learners, it is our duty to ask questions, share successes and challenges, and continue to tell stories for the benefit of ourselves, our peers, and ultimately our kids. Big or small, take on the challenge and *lurk no more*!

# RESOURCES

| LEARNING FROM THE WORLD KEY IDEAS | |
|---|---|
| **Become an Edu-Explorer!** | The world of education extends far beyond the walls of your classroom/site! Get out and look around. We guarantee you will find something you like! |
| **Develop your Tribe** | Seek out individuals who inspire, challenge, innovate, create, and push the boundaries of what you do! Where do you find these people? In your school, in your district, through a blog, in news articles, and on social media! |
| **Social Media Savvy** | Why seek out social media for professional gain rather than personal pleasure?<br><br>• Information-Seeking<br>• Professional Learning<br>• Connecting<br>• Idea-Generating<br><br>The world of social media is BIG. Be intentional with your consumption of information!<br><br>• Filter<br>• Edit<br>• Focus<br>• Balance |

# LEARN MORE FROM THOUGHT LEADERS WHO INSPIRE US TO LEARN FROM THE WORLD

## Read:

Aaker, J., & Smith, A. (2010). *The dragonfly effect: Quick, effective and powerful ways to use social media to drive social change.* San Francisco, CA: Jossey-Bass.

Dixon, B. (2012). *Social media for school leaders: A comprehensive guide to getting the most out of Facebook, Twitter, and other essential web tools.* San Francisco, CA: Jossey-Bass.

Heath, C., & Heath, D. (2010). *Switch: How to change things when change is hard.* New York, NY: Broadway Books.

Hord, S. M. (Ed.). (2004). *Learning together, leading together: Changing schools through professional learning communities.* New York, NY: Teachers College Press & NSDC.

Kleon, A. (2014). *Show your work!* New York, NY: Workman.

*Learning Forward Standards for Professional Learning: Resources, Data, and Implementation* (learningforward.org)

Magiera, J. (2016). *Courageous edventures: Navigating obstacles to discover classroom innovation.* Thousand Oaks, CA: Corwin.

## Watch:

Chitra Aiyar: How to Build Community When You Feel Isolated (2018). TED Talk (ted.com/talks/chitra_aiyar_ted_salon_belonging)

Eduardo Briceno: How to Get Better at the Things You Care About (2018). TEDx Talk (ted.com/talks/eduardo_briceno_how_to_get_better_at_the_things_you_care_about)

Richard Neville: How Can We Give Our Kids a Brighter Future? (2014). TED Talk (ted.com/talks/richard_neville_how_can_we_give_our_kids_a_brighter_future)

Rita Pierson: Every Kid Needs a Champion (2013). TED Talk (ted.com/talks/rita_pierson_every_kid_needs_a_champion)

## LEARN MORE FROM THOUGHT LEADERS WHO INSPIRE US TO LEARN FROM THE WORLD

### Listen:

The Ten-Minute Teacher podcast: coolcatteacher.com/podcast/

Infinite Thinking Machine podcast: infinitethinking.org/about.html

TeacherCast Education Network: teachercast.net/

Get Your Teach On LIVE: getyourteachon.com/category/gyto-live/

### Explore:

Estimation 180: www.estimation180.com

Hashtags (see pages 146–147)

TeachersConnect: teachersconnect.com

Visit evolvinglearning.org for more.

# THOUGHTS, JOTS, AND NEXT STEPS

# IN CLOSING

Throughout this book, we've examined professional learning from *kids*, *peers*, and *the world*. We have discussed the concept of learning through cycles of inquiry and the principle of equifinality, the reality that a cycle of inquiry for professional learning could look very different for two teachers and lead to the same positive results. Even if they teach the same subject, at the same grade level and at the same school, their cycle of inquiry could look different and still have the same positive impact. Understanding and appreciating this concept is critical in personalizing learning for adults.

Where are you in your professional learning journey? Start by considering the concept of professional development versus professional learning. One is externally driven, top-down, and one-size-fits-all. We know that this doesn't work well for kids, so why should adult learning be any different? Professional learning allows you to take back the reins and seek out what you *want* to learn and develop from. Living in an age where virtually anything we want to learn is at our fingertips, it is hard to believe that we have so few options for classroom teachers, instructional coaches/mentors, principals, and districtwide administrators to personalize their learning. To be fair, it is not entirely for lack of trying. There have been major financial investments in resources, from instructional coaches to technology. The problem is in the implementation. We implement fast and learn slow. Let's change that! A cycle of inquiry can also be used in designing professional learning experiences for a district, school, and team. The key is to be learner-focused throughout the entire process.

## Learning From Kids

As we have said before, kids are the most abundant resource in our schools. However, if we continually view them as being in a deficit role where adults provide all the guidance, information, and answers, how are we promoting inquiry and inspiring independence and leadership? Kids have a lot to say, and they can teach us in a variety of ways. When we, as educators and leaders, acknowledge and promote this, we drive self-efficacy and model that we are all learners at all times.

## Learning From Peers

Education, at times, can feel like an industry full of independent contractors. The traditional role of being the ruler of the classroom promotes the idea that teachers work alone and shut the door behind them when they begin to teach. While this is far from the truth, it can keep blinders on us to the wealth of knowledge we can source from someone who may work right next door. Learning from peers promotes collective efficacy and drives a culture of sharing. As the adage goes, "Sometimes the best PD [or in our case, PL] is the teacher down the hall."

## Learning From the World

One goal for this book was to help remove fear of the unknown for educators, coaches, and administrators. All three of us have at some point experienced fear and uncertainty in our careers, and it can be both immobilizing and demoralizing. It is this fear and uncertainty that breeds complacency and shuts down creativity and growth. It is the voice that tells us that we can, and should, only learn and grow from what is given to us or mandated for us. However, we all know this is not the truth. In the times that we live in, information, ideas, and connection are all around us, and we need only know how to access it and leverage it best. This book is meant to be one way to empower you and give you the tools to do just that. You are the driver in your professional learning and the journey of your career.

You entered this profession for a reason, and perhaps it is time to revisit that. What inspires you? How can you translate that into action? Who can help you? Where can you grow? You've always been a learner. All you need to continue to grow lies within connection, conversation, and inquiry with your kids, your peers, and the world of people and ideas who are here to help lift up and inspire you to transform the lives of kids. You are critical as the *Evolving Learner* who will continue to drive forward and push the boundaries toward better education for all, including yourself. You can learn from kids, peers, and the world!

# REFERENCES AND FURTHER READING

Aguilar, E. (2013). *The art of coaching: Effective strategies for school transformation.* San Francisco, CA: Wiley.

Aguilar, E. (2016). *The art of coaching teams: Building resilient communities that transform schools.* San Francisco, CA: Jossey-Bass.

Blackboard & Project Tomorrow. (2017). *Teachers' readiness to change instructional practices is top challenge to implementing educational technology.* Retrieved August 7, 2019, from https://tomorrow.org/pressroom/teachers-rediness-to-change-practices.html

Blanchard, K. H., & Johnson, S. (1994). *The one minute manager.* London, UK: HarperCollins.

Bloomberg, P., & Pitchford, B. (2017). *Leading impact teams: Building a culture of efficacy.* Thousand Oaks, CA: Corwin.

Brown, B. (2018). *Dare to lead: Brave work. Tough conversations. Whole hearts.* New York, NY: Random House.

Bryk, A. S., Gomez, L. M., Grunow, A., & LeMahieu, P. G. (2016). *Learning to improve: How America's schools can get better at getting better.* Cambridge, MA: Harvard Education Press.

Buck Institute for Education. (2019). *What is PBL?* Retrieved October 12, 2019, from https://www.pblworks.org/what-is-pbl

Center for Applied Special Technology (CAST). (2019, April 23). *CAST: About universal design for learning.* Retrieved August 7, 2019, from http://www.cast.org/our-work/about-udl.html#.XUs-c5NKjOQ

City, E. A., Elmore, R. F., Fiarman, S. E., Teitel, L., & Lachman, A. (2018). *Instructional rounds in education: A network approach to improving teaching and learning.* Cambridge, MA: Harvard Education Press.

Clayton Christensen Institute. (2019). *Blended Learning Universe: Basics.* Retrieved August 7, 2019, from https://www.blendedlearning.org/basics/

Collaborative for Academic, Social, and Emotional Learning (CASEL). (2019). *What is SEL?* Retrieved from https://casel.org/what-is-sel/

Crouch, C. H., & Mazur, E. (2001). *Peer instruction: Ten years of experience and results. American Journal of Physics, 69*(9), 970–977. https://doi.org/10.1119/1.1374249

Dana, N. F., Thomas, C. H., & Boynton, S. (2011). *Inquiry: A districtwide approach to staff and student learning.* Thousand Oaks, CA: Corwin, a joint publication with Learning Forward.

Dana, N. F., & Yendol-Hoppey, D. (2015). *The PLC book.* Thousand Oaks, CA: Corwin.

DuFour, R. (2004). *Whatever it takes: How professional learning communities respond when kids don't learn.* Bloomington, IN: National Education Service.

DuFour, R., DuFour, R., Eaker, R., & Many, T. (2006). *Learning by doing: A handbook for building professional learning communities.* Bloomington, IN: Solution Tree.

DuFour, R., & Eaker, R. (1998). *Professional learning communities at work: Best practices for enhancing student achievement.* Bloomington, IN: Solution Tree.

Hammond, Z. (2015). *Culturally responsive teaching and the brain: Promoting authentic engagement and rigor among culturally and linguistically diverse students.* Thousand Oaks, CA: Corwin.

Hattie, J. (2009). *Visible learning.* Thousand Oaks, CA: Corwin.

Hodges, T. (2018, October 25). *School engagement is more than just talk.* Retrieved August 7, 2019, from https://www.gallup.com/education/244022/school-engagement-talk.aspx

IIRP Staff. (2018). *Message from the president.* Retrieved October 22, 2019, from https://www.iirp.edu/restorative-practices/message-from-the-president

iNACOL. (2016, March 10). *What is competency education?* Retrieved August 7, 2019, from https://www.inacol.org/news/what-is-competency-education/

Jauhar, S. (2009). *Intern: A doctor's initiation.* New York, NY: Farrar, Straus & Giroux.

Joyce, B. R., & Showers, B. (1995). *Student achievement through staff development: Fundamentals of school renewal.* New York, NY: Longman.

Joyce, B. R., & Showers, B. (2002). *Student achievement through staff development.* Alexandria, VA: ASCD.

Kearsley, G. (2010). Andragogy (Malcolm Knowles). *The theory into practice database.* Retrieved from http://tip.psychology.org

Kleon, A. (2017, May 12). *Further Notes on scenius.* Retrieved August 7, 2019, from https://austinkleon.com/2017/05/12/scenius/

Knight, J. (2011). *Unmistakable impact: A partnership approach for dramatically improving instruction.* Thousand Oaks, CA: Corwin.

Knight, J. (2016). *Better conversations: Coaching ourselves and each other to be more credible, caring, and connected.* Thousand Oaks, CA: Corwin.

Knight, J. (2018). *The impact cycle: What instructional coaches should do to foster powerful improvements in teaching.* Thousand Oaks, CA: Corwin.

Knowles, M. (1984a). *The adult learner: A neglected species* (3rd ed.). Houston, TX: Gulf Publishing.

Knowles, M. (1984b). *Andragogy in action.* San Francisco, CA: Jossey-Bass.

Kuypers, L. M., & Winner, M. G. (2017). *The Zones of Regulation: A curriculum designed to foster self-regulation and emotional control.* Santa Clara, CA: Think Social.

Learning Forward. (2014). *A cycle of continuous improvement.* Retrieved from https://learningforward.org/docs/default-source/publicationssection/Transform/tool-cycle-of-continuous-improvement.pdf?sfvrsn=0

Le Fevre, D., Timperley, H., Twyford, K., & Ell, F. (2020). *Leading powerful professional learning: Responding to complexity with adaptive expertise.* Thousand Oaks, CA: Corwin.

MacDonald, E. (2013). *The skillful team leader: A resource for overcoming hurdles to professional learning for student achievement.* Thousand Oaks, CA: Corwin, a Joint Publication With Learning Forward.

Mitra, S. (2012, February 3). *The Hole in the Wall Project and the power of self-organized learning.* Retrieved August 7, 2019, from https://www.edutopia.org/blog/self-organized-learning-sugata-mitra

Mraz, K., Porcelli, A., & Tyler, C. (2016). *Purposeful play: A teacher's guide to igniting deep and joyful learning across the day.* Portsmouth, NH: Heinemann.

Resnick, M. (2017). *Lifelong kindergarten: Cultivating creativity through projects, passion, peers, and play.* Cambridge: The MIT Press.

Robinson, Sir K. (2009). *Changing education paradigms.* Retrieved August 7, 2019, from https://www.ted.com/talks/ken_robinson_changing_education_paradigms

Rothstein, D., & Santana, L. (2014). *Make just one change: Teach students to ask their own questions.* Cambridge, MA: Harvard Education Press.

RSA, The (2013). *Brené Brown on empathy.* Retrieved from https://www.youtube.com/watch?v=1Evwgu369Jw

Schechter, C. (2020). *The wisdom of practice: Leading learning from success.* Thousand Oaks, CA: Corwin.

Sheninger, E. C., & Murray, T. C. (2017). *Learning transformed: 8 keys to designing tomorrow's schools, today.* Alexandria, VA: ASCD.

Siegel, D. J. (2010). *Mindsight: The new science of personal transformation*. New York, NY: Bantam Books.

Siegel, D. J., & Bryson, T. P. (2012). *The whole-brain child: 12 revolutionary strategies to nurture your child's developing mind*. New York, NY: Bantam Books.

Svitak, A. (2010). *What adults can learn from kids*. Retrieved August 7, 2019, from https://www.ted.com/talks/adora_svitak?language=en

Svitak, A. (2012, July 23). *Dear parents: Leave us alone*. Retrieved August 7, 2019, from https://www.huffpost.com/entry/dear-parents-leave-us-alo_b_1666060

Sweeney, D. (2011). *Student-centered coaching: A guide for K–8 coaches and principals*. Thousand Oaks, CA: Corwin.

TNTP. (2015, August 4). *The mirage: Confronting the hard truth about our quest for teacher development*. Retrieved January 2, 2019, from https://tntp.org/publications/view/the-mirage-confronting-the-truth-about-our-quest-for-teacher-development

Toffler, A. (1970). *Future shock*. London, UK: Pan Books.

Tuckman, B. W. (1965). Developmental sequence in small groups. *Psychological Bulletin*, *63*(6), 384–399.

Walker, T. (2016, January 13). Global study: U.S. educators spend more hours teaching but wide pay gap remains. *NEA Today*. Retrieved August 7, 2019, from http://neatoday.org/2015/12/04/global-study-u-s-educators-spend-hours-teaching-wide-pay-gap-remains/

Wei, R. C., Darling-Hammond, L., Andree, A., Richardson, N., & Orphanos, S. (2009). *Professional learning in the learning profession: A status report on teacher development in the United States and abroad*. Dallas, TX: National Staff Development Council.

Will, M. (2019, May 14). What's harder than learning? Unlearning. *Education Week*. Retrieved August 7, 2019, from https://www.edweek.org/ew/articles/2019/05/15/whats-harder-than-learning-unlearning.html

Yale Center for Emotional Intelligence. (2015). *Emotion revolution—student*. Retrieved August 7, 2019, from http://ei.yale.edu/what-we-do/emotion-revolution-student/

# INDEX

A SAGE Publishing Company

**Helping educators make the greatest impact**

**CORWIN HAS ONE MISSION:** to enhance education through intentional professional learning.

We build long-term relationships with our authors, educators, clients, and associations who partner with us to develop and continuously improve the best evidence-based practices that establish and support lifelong learning.

## THE PROFESSIONAL LEARNING ASSOCIATION

Learning Forward is a nonprofit, international membership association of learning educators committed to one vision in K–12 education: Excellent teaching and learning every day. To realize that vision, Learning Forward pursues its mission to build the capacity of leaders to establish and sustain highly effective professional learning. Information about membership, services, and products is available from www.learningforward.org.

# Solutions YOU WANT | Experts YOU TRUST | Results YOU NEED

**EVENTS**

>>> **INSTITUTES**

Corwin Institutes provide large regional events where educators collaborate with peers and learn from industry experts. Prepare to be recharged and motivated!

**corwin.com/institutes**

**ON-SITE PD**

>>> **ON-SITE PROFESSIONAL LEARNING**

Corwin on-site PD is delivered through high-energy keynotes, practical workshops, and custom coaching services designed to support knowledge development and implementation.

**corwin.com/pd**

>>> **PROFESSIONAL DEVELOPMENT RESOURCE CENTER**

The PD Resource Center provides school and district PD facilitators with the tools and resources needed to deliver effective PD.

**corwin.com/pdrc**

**ONLINE**

>>> **ADVANCE**

Designed for K–12 teachers, Advance offers a range of online learning options that can qualify for graduate-level credit and apply toward license renewal.

**corwin.com/advance**

**Contact a PD Advisor at (800) 831-6640 or visit www.corwin.com for more information**